# THE MEANDERINGS
## OF A
## MEDITATIVE MIND

Alison Chant

THE MEANDERINGS
OF A
MEDITATIVE MIND

Alison Chant

For information on reordering, please contact:

Vision Publishing
P.O. Box 1680
Ramona, CA 92065
(760) 789-4700
www.booksbyvision.org

All scriptures New International Version
unless otherwise stated.

# Acknowledgement

I would like to thank Shannen Conlon for the artwork of the cover and the flowers.

# Table of Contents

# Foreword

In my old age, unable to minister as in times past through lack of energy, I determined to busy myself by meditating on Scripture during the Covid-19 lockdown. This idea has kept me occupied now for over a year and I hope has produced some helpful ideas for Christians who worship the Father, love the Lord Jesus, and enjoy the fellowship of the Holy Spirit.

A few of these meditations were written in past years but the bulk have been written during the year I turned 87 years of age in the June of 2021. I pray the Lord will bless you as you read through them and contemplating them will perhaps inspire you to write some meditations on the Word of God for yourself.

This book is set out with various Scriptures followed by a meditation arising from that Scripture. They are written in no particular order so are truly *The Meanderings of a Meditative Mind*.

*Rejoice always, pray continually, give thanks in all circumstances; for this is God's will for you in Christ Jesus* (1Thessalonians 5:16-17).

**Heavenly Father,**
I sit and dream of the great universe,
and of your immense power.
The beauty and the majesty of your creation,
both in the microcosm and the macrocosm,
leaves little room for negative thoughts.

The smallest flower and the highest mountain
in their different ways set forth your splendour,
King of kings, and Lord of lords.

Create in me a clean heart O Lord,
forgive any sins I have committed,
some of which I may be unaware.
Help me to live a life of repentance
and true holiness in your eyes.

Show me anything in my life
that is not pleasing to you.
Change me where I need to change,
that I may be ready to meet you
when you come again for your church.
Amen.

# A Song of Joy

*Sing to the LORD, for he has done glorious things; let this be known to all the world. Shout aloud and sing for joy, people of Zion, for great is the Holy One of Israel among you* (Isaiah 12:5-6).

Sing and shout for joy, people of God.
Rejoice with all your heart,
You who love him.
For the Lord has given you a new start,
Removing your sins far from you.
The Lord, the King of kings, is with you.

There is no reason now to fear,
You are freed by his mighty power,
Because of Calvary's grace.
There he poured out his great love shower,
And filled you with his joy,
Joy that now overflows into praise.

So, praise the Lord, give glory to him
For he is your protection.
Sing to him, sing praises
For his powerful and glorious resurrection.
Worship his Kingly Majesty
Enthroned forever in everlasting light.[1]

---

[1] This Psalm was inspired by a pastor who challenged Christians to write a Psalm

Rejoice in the Lord always.
I will say it again: Rejoice!
(Philippians 4:4)


**Heavenly Father**, thank you that we can worship and adore you and rejoice in your love and mercy each day. Help us to worship you with psalms and hymns and spiritual songs, making melody in our heart and with our voice. We rejoice, both in the great salvation you have given us and the love you shower upon us. May our worship be pleasing to you. Amen.

# Summertime

*The Lord will guide you always; he will satisfy your needs in a sun scorched land and will strengthen your frame. You will be like a well-watered garden, like a spring whose waters never fail* (Isaiah 58:11).

Over twenty years ago, while we were living in the USA, our good friend Rev. Dick Mills prophesied that one day we would be living in a two-story house in Sydney. As it happened, we were back in Australia and living in our house for quite a while before we remembered the prophecy. Then we rejoiced at the accuracy of God's word to us and the timing of it as our house has indeed two-stories and is located in a suburb of Sydney.

We also rejoiced because we feel so safe here. The storms that hit Sydney seem to miss us completely. We live at the foot of the Blue Mountains and the violent storms coming from the mountains seem to pass right over us and land on areas nearer the sea. Here we are safe and secure in our old age and can testify that God is no man's debtor. He has provided for us, and we have lived here tranquilly for the past twenty-five years. Before that, because of our ministry, we moved at least twenty-seven times and lived in four different states of Australia, and two different countries, our homeland and the USA.

Today is a beautiful summers day, the sun is shining, and the garden is blooming. October is the best month for our garden when all the flowers are at their most extravagant in size, colour and profusion.

This morning I have been given the task of clearing the flowers that are beginning to droop to make room for more to grow. This is the way of all life in this world of ours. We humans, like the flowers, have our time to flourish and then fade into old age, giving room for others in their turn to make their mark on the world.

As Moses declared in his prayer in Psalm 90, "*Our days may come to seventy years, or eighty, if our strength endures.*" Though nowadays, because of the advances of modern medicine, some even live to ninety or even one hundred years. But it is always sad when someone dies at a comparatively young age, before fulfilling their dreams.

I remember when our beloved son-in-law, David, died suddenly we were all devastated. His ministry, especially in India, was greatly appreciated and was sadly missed when he passed away. I asked the Lord for comfort and understanding, and he showed me a verse in Job which satisfied me at the time. "*A person's days are determined; you have decreed the number of his months and have set limits he can't exceed*" (Job 14:5).

As Christians we all have our moment to depart and be with the Lord, and because he knows the future he knows when our time will come. We cannot die until God decrees, but when that time comes our limit has been set and it is our time to go.

So, while we enjoy the beauty of our garden in the summer-time, we know that its fragile flowers are temporal, and the beauties of heaven far outweigh the colourful scenery we enjoy here.

Now, as my husband and I grow old together, getting ever closer to our ninetieth year, we know the happiness we enjoy here on this earth will be far surpassed by the bliss of our journey into heaven's glory. There we will experience the joy of dwelling with God and his mighty angels and of walking and talking with Jesus our Saviour.

**Heavenly Father**, thank you for providing for us in our old age. Thank you for the loving family that surrounds us. We pray that we will always walk in your will and complete the work you have given us to do before we go to be with you for ever. We pray for our loved ones, that you will speak to them in the quiet moments and show them your great love. May they all finally surrender their lives into your keeping. Amen.

# He is Wonderful

*The heavens declare the glory of God; the skies proclaim the work of his hands. Day after day they pour forth speech; night after night they reveal knowledge* (Psalm 19:1-2).

Our Mathematical God reveals himself
In leafy trees and flowers.
Showing exquisite formation
In his grand creation.

Our Artistic God spreads many colours,
Yellow gold, orange and grey.
He paints perfect sunsets high
In the vault of the sky.

Our Amazing God spreads his healing
In plants, herbs, and fauna.
Discoveries reward with health
Those who seek this wealth.

Our God reveals himself in many ways.
Be aware, discover his care.
Protection is ours
If we trust in his power.

The Holy Spirit descends as a dove.
Search for him, nor rest until
You are enfolded above
In his perfect love.

**Heavenly Father**, thank you for loving us with a great and everlasting love. Thank you for the wonderful world you have given us to enjoy and for the beauty of your creation. Thank you for giving us your precious Holy Spirit of wisdom and revelation, so that we may learn to know you better. Thank you that you care for us and watch over us and that we can cast our cares and anxieties on you and thank you for your protection for us and our loved ones. Amen

# Seeing God in the Ordinary

*God's glory is on tour in the skies, God-craft on exhibit across the horizon. Madame Day holds classes every morning, Professor Night lectures each evening* (Ps.19:1 Message Bible).

Motoring along the Pacific highway one evening, my husband and I were struck by the beautiful silhouettes of the trees against the evening sky. How peaceful and uplifting are those moments when God seems very close. While observing the trees I was led to a complex thought. "Why doesn't God open the sky and let us see him in all his glory? Then all men would fall down and worship him."

I posed this question to my husband and his answer was, "God doesn't reveal himself because he has granted us free will. If we could see him, if he did not veil his face, then there would be no free choice to believe or not to believe. We would all know without a doubt that God is sovereign."

I realised in that moment God must also have veiled his glory and complete authority from his angels in the beginning. Otherwise, Satan would not have thought he could challenge God and take his place, and a third of the angels would not have fallen with him.

> God is everywhere visible in his
> creation and there is no excuse for
> those who deny him

Yes, it is true God has hidden his greater glory from us, but I am daily seeing signs of God's presence around me. In forest trees, beautiful sunsets, a rose, a desert flower, or in a new-born baby. God is everywhere visible in his creation and there is no excuse for those who deny him. He can be seen clearly in the smallest creature, in the tallest trees, in the birds, the bees and the towering mountain heights.

If you are a Christian, then he is within you through his Holy Spirit. But, if at times you do not feel his presence, if you feel God is far away from you, look for him in the ordinary, in his creation that is all around you.

Take time to contemplate a daisy, listen to the song of the magpie, look for God in all that is beautiful and charming in this world. When you do you will strengthen your awareness of God and, in the joy of seeing and acknowledging his creation, you will once again feel his presence near you.

He has promised in his Word to be closer to you than a brother, and when it is your time to go to be with him forever, he will be waiting to greet you.

**Heavenly Father**, thank you for this beautiful world you have given us to enjoy. Thank you for the wonderful and complex creatures you have made and the lovely flowers and trees. Thank you that we can see you in your creation. How marvellous are your works and your ways past finding out. Help us to see you in the ordinary things of life and appreciate all you have done to reveal yourself to us. Amen

# The Sword of the Lord

*For the word of God is alive and active. Sharper than any double-edged sword, it penetrates even to dividing soul and spirit, joints and marrow; it judges the thoughts and attitudes of the heart* (Hebrews 4:12).

Like lightning his Word falls.
From eternity it calls,
As an incandescent flame.
Powerful on the Narrow Way,
It rewards those who claim
In Jesus' name to pray.

Its treasures hide patiently
For those who determinedly
Discover its vastness.
While they study the Word,
Light pierces the darkness
And wields the Sword.

Guidance awaits careful
Students who are prayerful,
Who seek to know and understand
The flow of revelation
Written long ago.
In God's mercy we grow.

Wise men seek earnestly,
Passages of certainty
Only God bestows.
Amazingly, right thinking
Enlightens and overflows
Into revelation dynamite.

**Heavenly Father**, thank you that Jesus our Saviour is the radiance of your glory and the exact representation of your being. Thank you that he holds all things together by his powerful word and that finally every knee will bow before him to acknowledge him as King of kings, and Lord of lords. Thank you for your Word that reveals Jesus as your One and Only Son who was willing to die on the cross for us all. Amen

# The Beauty and the Glory

*The fruit of the Spirit is love, joy, peace, forbearance, kindness, goodness, faithfulness, gentleness, and self-control* (Galatians 5:22-23).

Many months ago, I planted some Lilium bulbs. Small and brown and wrinkled they held no hint of the beauty that lay within. Today, two of them have bloomed and I am enjoying their delicate colours and exquisitely formed petals. I have waited patiently all these months and today I am rewarded.

Do the fruits of the Spirit appear
to the Lord in colour?

Knowing that eventually they would bloom, I have examined them each day to see, first the struggling green shoots, then the stalks growing tall, the buds slowly forming and swelling, and then finally the finished flower in all its perfection.

I like to think that the Lord hovers over us as I hovered over my bulbs, waiting to see how we will develop. Will all his patient care bear the good fruit for which he is looking? Will we change from something less than beautiful yet full of promise, to something that will gladden the heart of the Father?

What colour is love?

I wonder do the fruits of the Spirit appear to the Lord in colour? If they do, then what colour is Love? I think it must be pink, for Love is warm. And Joy; something vibrant and full of life, such as red. What colour is Peace? Surely it is white? One could go on...

Our God is such a creative God. The variety there is in nature never ceases to amaze me. And God is so prolific! He creates beauty in places where mortals may never go; in the secret places of the earth; in thick jungle; on remote mountain peaks. Also, in places that we cannot see without a microscope. In these places he creates beauty that may never be seen except by the heavenly host.

Many wonderful things are being discovered in our day. Plants that are good for medicine; new species; new creatures. Some of these created by God long ago are only now being found and used to benefit mankind. Surely, we worship a wonderful, marvellous God.

> Let us glory in our great God;
> in his creation; in his tender care
> of us; in the salvation he has provided
> for us and in the hope
> we have of eternal life.

The God we worship, who creates such beauty, must himself be more glorious than anything we can imagine. In the words of the Psalmist –

*One thing I ask of the Lord, this is what I seek: That I may dwell in the house of the Lord all the days of my life, to gaze upon the beauty of the Lord and to seek him in his temple (Psalm 27:4).*[2]

Let us then glory in our great God; in his creation; in his tender care of us; in the salvation he has provided for us; in the hope we have of eternal life. Let us look forward to the day we can worship in his temple with all those who love his appearing.

**Heavenly Father**, thank you for the fact that one day we will dwell with you forever and be able to join with the angels in worshiping you. Thank you for your protection while we are in this world, thank you for the Holy Spirit's guidance as we walk with you and talk with you each day. We pray that you will be pleased with us as we continue our Christian walk of obedience to your voice and seek to grow more like Jesus, day by day. Amen

---

[2] Published first in *Rebecca's Reflections*

# Eternity

*Have the same mind set as Christ Jesus; Who, being in very nature God, did not consider equality with God something to be used to his own advantage; rather, he made himself nothing by taking the very nature of a servant, being made in human likeness, and being found in appearance as a man, he humbled himself by becoming obedient to death – even death on a cross! Therefore, God exalted him to the highest place and gave him the name that is above every name, that at the name of Jesus every knee should bow, in heaven and on earth and under the earth, and every tongue acknowledge that Jesus Christ is Lord, to the glory of God the Father* (Philippians 2:5b-11).

Child of eternity,
Suckled in infancy,
Mary thus fulfilling her destiny.

Son of the Father,
Healer deliverer,
Jesus, Saviour divinely inspired.

Came as a servant,
Humble indignity,
Nailed to a cross, liberating humanity.

Now raised in glory,
Seated in Majesty,
And interceding for settled security.

King of all other kings,
Reigning in Authority,
Mission completed, resting in victory.

**Heavenly Father**, we acknowledge the glory of your One and Only Son, Jesus our Saviour. He was the firstborn over all creation. In him all things were created, in heaven and in earth, visible and invisible. How wonderful he is to us, so loving and kind yet full of Majesty and Authority as King of kings, and Lord of lords. Now to this King eternal, immortal, invisible, the only God, be honour and glory forever and ever. Amen

# A Bridal Psalm

*A wife of noble character who can find? She is worth far more than rubies* (Proverbs 31:10).

Thank you, God for this world and all its beauty,
For the majesty of the high mountains and
For the valleys with their mighty rivers.
Thank you for the morning star and
The sunrise of another day,
For tranquil evenings and velvet darkness.
All creation joins me in singing praise to your name.

Thank you, God for the husband you have given me,
For his gentleness, his sensitivity, his inner strength
And delightful sense of humour.
Thank you for the years we will share
Together with you, and for love
That is giving and doing and tender and joyful.
All creation joins me in singing praise to your name.

Thank you, God for making me a woman,
How blessed I am that you have given me
The ability to bear a child.
Nourishing and caring for my family will reveal to me
A little of your love for me.
Grant me insight I pray into your infinite love.
All creation joins me in singing praise to your name.

Thank you, God for the joy that will be ours
In the years that lie ahead.
For the little things, the precious memories
And the opportunities to serve you together.
Thank you for the trials, causing us to grow in wisdom
And the ability to share the things we learn.
All creation joins me in singing praise to your name.[3]

**Heavenly Father**, thank you for marriage and family and the happiness this can bring. Help us to be kind and loving and forgiving within the family circle. We thank you for predestining us for adoption to sonship through Jesus Christ, and for making us part of your family. Amen.

---

[3] Written in Tasmania circa 1966.

# The Beauty of Creation

*For he has made everything beautiful in its time. He has also set eternity in the human heart; yet no one can fathom what God has done from beginning to end* (Ecclesiastes 3:11).

God has created much that is breathtakingly beautiful in this world of ours. Lakes that mirror glorious sunsets and clouds that float in the sky above them. Snow covered mountains towering in the distance, stark against the deep blue of the sky. Autumn leaves and the heavy snows of winter. Icicles hanging from the trees and gables that glitter with a thousand rainbow colours in the winter sunshine.

These I believe were created by God to appeal to our better selves, to lift us from this earthly realm into an awareness of his glory and beauty.

We spent five years in Minnesota USA and saw and enjoyed all these sights even though the cold was bitter, sometimes 50 degrees below zero because of the wind chill. We couldn't go outside the house without wearing proper warm clothing and covering our mouth and nose to protect us from the freezing cold breezes.

The heat from one candle
could keep us alive

One winter night we were driving home and thinking how romantic the moonlight looked shining on the snow. We were shocked out of our musings when the car broke down. But we had prepared for a time like this and took a candle from the glove compartment and set it alight. We had been advised that the heat from one candle would be enough to keep us alive and soon we did feel warm and comfortable.

To our relief it was not long before the police, out looking for breakdowns, drove up and explained to us that the car fuel pipe was probably frozen. If we waited a few minutes, it would unfreeze, and we would be able to drive home. This proved true and we were greatly relieved to get to our destination safely.

Many times, during our five years in Minnesota God rescued us and kept us from accidents and injuries for which we thank and praise him. He is a good God.

However, we were glad after those five years to have an invitation to move to California where it was almost always warm and sunny!

After spending ten years in the United States during the eighties, we returned to our homeland of Australia, and we can testify of the goodness of God over our lifetime. In moments of joy and gladness and in moments of sadness we know the Lord has been near to share his love and protection with us.

However, not every land enjoys the peace and safety we enjoy in Australia, and we feel for those who are suffering persecution in other countries. Persecution is worst in Muslim and Communist countries and in this last one hundred years, more martyrs have been killed for their faith than in all Christian history combined.

There are some mysteries in the Christian life, why some are protected from danger and life-threatening circumstances, and some are not, but we know that God will compensate those who suffer now. Their reward will be great in heaven, and they will have a better resurrection as we read in Hebrews:

*There were others who were tortured, refusing to be released so that they might gain an even better resurrection* (Hebrews 11:35b).

**Heavenly Father**, thank you for keeping us safe so many times. We pray for continued peace in this land and for a return to peace in the world in which we live. We pray for Christians in other countries who are in danger and in fear of persecution and death unless they deny you. We pray that you will give those who are in danger the courage to endure. And we pray that you will continue to grow your underground church wherever it is flourishing despite persecution. Amen

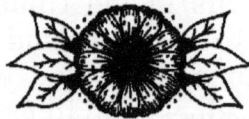

# A Psalm of Praise

*Praise be to the God and Father of our Lord Jesus Christ, who has blessed us in the heavenly realms with every spiritual blessing in Christ* (Ephesians 1:3).

Praise Jesus in the heavenlies.
Praise him at God's right hand.
Praise him for his power and glory.
Praise him for healing and miracles.
Praise him for free salvation.
Praise him for rivers of living water.
Praise him with tongues of men and angels.
Praise him for Holy Spirit baptism.
Praise him for sending our Counsellor who leads
and guides us.
For all these things let us praise him.
Praise the Lord.
Praise Jesus for enduring the cross.
Praise him for his obedience unto death.
Praise him for the power of his resurrection.
Praise him for Holy Spirit baptism.
Praise him for fruits of righteousness.
Praise him for the good work he has done.
Praise him for giving us courage to live for him.
Praise him for his precious promises.
Praise him for answers to prayer and the joy set before us.
For all these things let us praise him.
Praise the Lord.

**Heavenly Father**, thanks and praise be unto your name forever more. You are great and greatly to be praised. Thank you for keeping us safe from the enemy of our souls and for your promise to bring us safely into your presence when the time comes. Thank you for answering our prayers and petitions and for giving us a heavenly language with which to worship and praise you daily. Amen

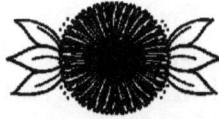

# An Acrostic Psalm

*It is good to praise the Lord and make music to your name, O Most High, proclaiming your love in the morning and your faithfulness at night* (Psalm 92:1-2).

Arise and let us go into the house of the Lord,
for there is light and life and joy.

Behold my Lord and my Redeemer,
in him I rest, obedient to his commands.

Come and let us worship him in unity,
for that is powerful and pleasing to God.

Desire fills my heart for my Lord,
for he is the lover of my soul.

Each day he draws closer to me,
as I reach out in adoration to him.

For he is my strong fortress, my hiding place,
in him I am safe from my enemies.

God is my help at all times,
though I fall he will lift me up.

He is the strength of my life,
with him I shall never be afraid.

Infinite is his wisdom and knowledge,
he will lead me safely through dark places.

Jesus is my Saviour and my King,
as he strengthens me, I will serve him

Keep me on the highway of holiness,
do not let me stray from your pathway.

Lead me in the way everlasting,
and I will praise you for your guiding hand.

My heart is fixed on my God,
for he is all I need now and evermore.

No weapon that is formed against me shall prosper,
while my God is with me.

O taste and see that the Lord is good,
his pleasures are to be enjoyed without regret.

Powerful and Majestic is the Lord my God,
he dwells within me helping me along.

Quietly I rest in the Lord my God,
knowing he will keep me safe from harm.

Remember, the Lord keeps his word to you,
you can trust him always.

Swiftly he will come to your aid,
all you need to do is call him by name.

Touch him and he will touch you,
in blessing and healing power.

Underneath his wings he will gather you,
to protect you from your enemies.

Victory will be yours as you fight for him,
and he will not leave you comfortless.

Wonderful is his love toward you,
he will never leave you nor forsake you.

Xylophones with orchestras make beautiful
music giving praise to his Majesty

Yield yourself to the Lord,
and he will grant you joy everlasting.

Zeal for your God will consume you,
and your reward will be life eternal.

**Heavenly Father**, thank you for your precious Word that is a light to our path and for the guidance it gives. We know that you will be with us and grant us more and more insight and revelation as we study your Word. Help us to explore the wonderful gifts you have poured out on your church and to claim those we need for our ministry to others. Amen.

# A Christmas Legend

*(Joseph) got up, took the child and his mother during the night, and left for Egypt, where he stayed until the death of Herod. And so was fulfilled what the Lord had said through the prophet: "Out of Egypt I called my Son"* (Matthew 2:14-15).

Many years ago, I heard a legend about Joseph and Mary's flight to Egypt with the baby Jesus.

Now a legend is not a true story; but may have its roots in truth. It is a story told over and over until it takes on the mantle of truth. Then it becomes a legend. This story may not have any foundation in truth, but even if it has not, it is still a lovely story illustrating the power of God to protect the Christmas family from the cruelty of King Herod.

The legend begins with the hasty exit of Joseph and Mary from Bethlehem with baby Jesus. They left quickly and quietly at the warning of the messenger angel. Probably they had a donkey for Mary and the baby and, in their bundles of clothing, would have rested the wealth given to them by the Wise Men. This gold, frankincense and myrrh would be so necessary when they arrived in Egypt and shows the deliberate and careful planning of the Father in providing for this little family.

After travelling a long way, they thought that they were safely distant from Bethlehem and could stop for a while. They found a cave and bedded down for some rest. During the night God prepared a spider to make a thick web over the cave opening. Next day some of the Soldiers with orders from the king to kill all the boy babies under two years of age began searching the area. They marched past the cave and Joseph and Mary prayed that the baby Jesus and the donkey would remain quiet.

One of the soldiers started toward the cave but his commander shouted, "Don't bother with that cave, can't you see there is a thick spider's web over the opening? There cannot be anyone in there."

Thankfully and with hearts rejoicing in the goodness and mercy of God, Mary and Joseph gave a sigh of relief. Soon the soldiers had marched away back toward Bethlehem and the holy family were able to continue their journey to Egypt and safety.

**Heavenly Father**, thank you for taking care of the Holy family when they were journeying to Egypt. Thank you for supplying them with the riches they needed to survive there. The gold, frankincense and myrrh given to Baby Jesus by the wise men were your provision for their future journey. You provided for them in the past and you are still providing for your children today. Thank you for the many times you make provision for us when we cry out to you for help. Amen

# The Sound of Many Waters

*In the beginning God created the heavens and the earth*
(Genesis 1:1).

For blue grey skies above and
Mint green seas below,
For the beauty of creation
We give you thanks O Lord

Like the sound of many waters
Our voices lift in praise,
For the many blessings granted
We give you thanks O Lord.

For majestic running rivers
And thundering waterfalls,
For quiet streams and lakes
We give you thanks O Lord.

For family and faithful friends
And happy joyful children,
For tranquil resting places
We give you thanks O Lord.

**Heavenly Father**, thank you that you are our Shepherd and that we lack no good thing your hand can provide. Thank you for leading us beside quiet waters and for refreshing our soul as we wait in your presence. Thank you for being with us in the good times and in the sorrowful times and for the knowledge that we can turn to you any time we need your help. Amen

# God's Love

*When you pass through the waters, I will be with you; and when you pass through the rivers, they will not sweep over you. When you walk through the fire, you will not be burned; the flames will not set you ablaze. For I am the Lord your God, the Holy One of Israel, your Saviour* (Isaiah 43:2-3a).

Pass through the waters,
And swim in the rivers,
They will not drown you.
You will be upheld, you won't falter
For Jesus is a victorious Saviour.

Walk through the fire,
And the cleansing flames,
They will not burn you.
A caring Jesus lifts from the ashes,
That is the reason he came.

When you are suffering,
Jesus comes swiftly,
Showing his love to you.
For today, tomorrow and forever,
He carries you carefully.

When depression clings,
Causing you great harm,
He will strengthen you.
You will not die, but sing victoriously
Of joy and peace in a psalm.

Your courage breaks
Chains of stubborn resistance,
Then freedom comes to you.
God's abundant and unfailing love
Proclaims a time of deliverance.


**Heavenly Father**, thank you that the angel of the Lord encamps around those who fear him, and delivers them. Thank you that we can taste and see that you are good and that you bless those who take refuge in you. You are a strong tower, a mighty fortress, and we can run to you when we are afraid and need courage to face the future. Help us to remember this always. Amen

# Seek Wisdom

*Go to the ant, you sluggard; consider its ways and be wise! It has no commander, no overseer or ruler, yet it stores its provisions in summer and gathers its food at harvest* (Proverbs 6:6-8).

We are bidden to learn wisdom from one of God's smallest creatures. The writer of Proverbs speaks with scorn of those who are lazy and do not make provision for their future.

Recently we had an invasion of small black ants, and I was going to spray them. However, my daughter, who also had an invasion, had been watching the ants and she noticed that they sent out a few scouts first to find the way to the food source.

Normally these scouts report back to the main army who arrive to glean what they can from our scraps. Sharon discovered that if she swept up these scouts and put them outside then they became confused and could not correctly show the way to the food source. This meant she had no more ants coming into her kitchen. Surely a more humane way of dealing with the invasion!

Ants are indeed wonderful creatures, if one ant finds something too big to handle it will go to find another ant to help. The two touch feelers, just as if they are talking together and then they move the titbit between them. You can discover many wonderful things about ants. What remarkable creatures they are. They cooperate together, build nests, and care for each other.

They know how to find food and they are capable of moving things far larger than themselves. The writer of proverbs spoke truly when he advised us to look at the ants, and to learn from them not to be lazy! They are indeed busy little creatures, showing great wisdom!

Ants have a unique food chamber system, and this is achieved by using certain ants in the colony called 'Repletes'. These Repletes are fed food which they keep in their specially designed 'social stomach'. This they distribute when needed to worker ants.

Honeypot ants store honey in their body and when food is scarce other ants stroke them slowly, thus releasing the honey for food.

Army Ants carry their food in bulk till they build a living nest by every ant linking up, and then they distribute the food. Truly remarkable little creatures, showing the wonders of God's creation.

**Heavenly Father**, thank you for giving us the illustration of the ants to warn us not to be lazy. Help us to look ahead and make provision for the future, for ourselves and our children. Assist us to build strong families and to teach our children the satisfaction of work well done. Amen

# An Australian Psalm

*Sing to the LORD a new song; sing to the LORD all the earth. Sing to the LORD, praise his name; proclaim his salvation day after day. Declare his glory among the nations, his marvellous deeds among all peoples* (Psalm 96:1-3).

The lonely stars shine in beauty,
Singing serenely to God who created them from nothing.
The blazing sun rises to a new day,
And in the distant horizon appears
The circle of the earth.

Far to the north clouds burst, dry creek beds run,
Filled with swelling, sparkling, life-giving water.
Kangaroos and wallabies come to drink gratefully,
While desert flowers bend in the gentle breeze.

Eager birds follow, flying by your decree O Lord
To feast right royally.
Newly fledged birds praise God constantly.
With joyous cacophony.

Truly, you are a good God,
You make the desert blossom as a rose
Even as you promised long ago.
You sustain life and care lovingly for your creation
In the lonely places.

Your glory endures forever.
I will sing songs of the beauty of the Lord
And dwell in his courts forever.
May my meditation be pleasing to him
In the night watches.[4]

**Heavenly Father**, thank you for the wonders of your world. May our praise be acceptable to you who are the Artistic creator. We see your glory in golden sunsets, in craggy mountains and in the stunning flower displays in summer-time gardens around us. You are a good God who supplies food for all your creation. Thank you for the rainbow and your promise not to flood the earth again. And thank you for your promise to keep us safe as we trust in you. Amen

[4] Published in *Life of Balance* 2020

# The Splendour of His Holiness

*Ascribe to the LORD the glory due his name; worship the LORD in the splendour of his holiness* (Psalm 29:2)

Lord, we worship you for the wonders and the beauty and the power of your creation. When we think of the mighty mountains, the crackling, and booming of a lightning storm, the thunder of waterfalls that sweep all before them and then contrast these with the beauty of a small and fragile flower we are amazed at the complexity of your creation and the depths of your abilities that are far beyond our understanding. We praise you for being the great Architect for we see in nature the proof of your designing genius.

We respect you and honour you for you are a great and powerful being. Yet we know that you are also a God who is slow to anger and full of mercy and that you love us. We are grateful for this as we know that if you did not love us, we would be undone.

We thank you because you have made it possible for us to worship you in spirit and in truth. If not for your mercy in sending Jesus, your one and only Son, to die in our place we could not dare to come before you to worship you. Thank you for his precious blood which cleanses us from all our sin and helps us live for you.

Thank you for all the blessings you have given us. A place to live in peace, family and friends to enjoy, with all earthly needs met.

Many in this world do not have our blessings. Their families are torn apart by war, they have to leave their homes and possessions. They suffer hunger and cold. They live in tents with insufficient water and food. I know that you love them too, as you love all mankind, and I thank you for the men and women you have inspired to spend their lives helping these desperate refugees. One day there will be no more suffering or tears of despair and no more war, because you will be in charge of all things, and you do all things well.

**Heavenly Father**, we know that the kind of religion that pleases you is the religion that cares for the widows and the orphans in their distress. You have told us to give to the poor and those who are in need and to be kind to those who are refugees from war. These things are pleasing to you. Help us to always please you in everything we do. Amen

# A Meditation on Heaven

*Our citizenship is in heaven. And we eagerly await a Saviour from there, the Lord Jesus Christ, who, by the power that enables him to bring everything under his control, will transform our lowly bodies so that they will be like his glorious body* (Philippians 3:20-21).

As heaven is where Jesus is,
Jesus is where heaven is!
Because Jesus is closer than a brother,
With us to the end of the age,
And dwelling in us through his Holy Spirit,
Heaven is closer than we think!

Because we are earth bound, we cannot see the glories
Of heaven with our eyes,
Nor hear its beautiful music with our ears,
But they are there none the less.
God is there with Jesus, and his mighty angels,
And the saints who have served him victoriously.

If God were to open our eyes to see and our ears to hear
We would be amazed at the glory surrounding us!
Because of this our loved ones who have gone to
be with Jesus
Are closer than we can imagine,
There is only a veil between.

We can look forward to being able to see them
Because heaven is more real than this world of ours.
Earth's mountains, and seas, and abundant trees and flowers
Are ephemeral and insubstantial by comparison,
A vapour that will one day pass away.

Heaven is real and true; more solid than the things we see
With our eyes and touch with these hands of ours.
Its music more wonderful than any we hear on earth.
Jesus our Saviour is heaven's glorious King, and he has
Promised to prepare a place for us there.

As we grow older, we dream of heaven and of walking
And talking with Jesus.
Even though we may be a small and humble part of his plan,
We know he will have time for us,
Because he is present everywhere,
And available to anyone who needs him.

Heaven feels very near when our loved ones go before us.
They will stand with Jesus at heaven's gate
To greet us when we come.
We don't know how they will appear,
But we will know them instantly
As they wait to welcome us into heaven's glory.
There we will be together forever. Amen![5]

**Heavenly Father**, thank you for Jesus our Saviour and the salvation he has provided for us. One day we know we will see heaven and your majestic throne room where you are seated with Jesus at your right hand. There we will join your mighty angels and the redeemed saints singing and worshiping you with overwhelming joy. We look forward to that great day and of walking and talking with Jesus. Amen

[5] Written after the death of a loved one and published in *Life of Balance* 2020

# Emotions

*Finally, brothers and sisters, whatever is true, whatever is noble, whatever is right, whatever is pure, whatever is lovely, whatever is admirable – if anything is excellent or praiseworthy – think about such things* (Philippians 4:8).

Our emotions have no will of their own
They merely follow our will,
Our thoughts and our decisions.
Therefore, we will not think about the past
Which we cannot change,
Nor the future,
For it has not yet arrived.
Instead, we will enjoy the present moment,
God's beautiful creation,
And those we love.
Our emotions will come into line
With our will, and decisions we make,
Changing to reflect our thoughts.
They are now positive instead of negative,
Happy and cheerful,
Instead of sad and miserable.
Loving instead of unloving.
Forgiving instead of un-forgiving.
We will cease to brood and begin to live,
Victoriously in Christ.[6]

---

[6] Published in *Life of Balance* 2020

**Heavenly Father**, thank you for the wisdom of your Word and that we can come to you and ask for that wisdom when we need it. Thank you that you are always willing to listen to our petitions and to give us wisdom and understanding when we need to make an important decision. Thank you for showing us how to live, in ways that will please you. Help us to be obedient to the still small voice of your Holy Spirit each day. Amen

# Gratitude

*I will remember the deeds of the LORD; yes, I will remember your miracles of long ago. I will consider all your works and meditate on all your mighty deeds* (Psalm 77:11-12).

The other day I heard a man say he thanks God every morning for 300 blessings, I was amazed! Surely, there are not that many we can claim each day? I decided to see how many I could think of for which to thank the Lord.

First of course, is the Lord himself, and the blessing he bestows on us by his loving kindness. How blessed we are that he gave himself so freely to redeem us. He favours us too, by the spiritual guidance he gives, and the comfort when we are sore distressed.

Then there are the angels, sent to minister to us at God's decree. Both Ken and I have been saved from death more than once during our lifetime. I'm sure God has kept us safe because he had a job for us to complete. We are grateful for our guardian angels otherwise each of us would have died in our teenage years. Then in the first two years of our marriage in a potential car accident, which we narrowly escaped. God is good.

Then we need to be grateful for family members. Spouse, sisters, brothers, in-laws, children, grandchildren and great grandchildren, nieces, nephews, cousins. Calling them all by name would cover many more.

We also appreciate our helpful adult children who love us. Then there are friends of many years standing, though we don't see much of each other now, we look forward to being together in eternity. This gives me at least another twenty or thirty for which to be grateful. Our church family comes next in line, especially those who are most precious in friendship to us.

Refreshing weeks of rain in answer
to united prayer have put out the
bushfires of the year 2020

Then there are the beauties of nature, the lovely trees and flowers with all their different colours and delicate and exquisite scents, delighting our senses. God has given us the rivers, the lakes, and the sea to enjoy, all from his bounty. The beauty of the mountains with their eternal ice and freezing snow are essential. A world without water would be our doom.

For refreshing weeks of rain in answer to united prayer which have put out the bushfires of this year 2020.

There is still more to be grateful for in our daily round, a home in which to live, though many have lost theirs in the bushfires we can be grateful ours still stands. Then we have clean water to drink, hot showers and uncontaminated food.

We are blessed with electricity, which provides a refrigerator to keep our food fresh, a washing machine to clean our clothes, and other power tools which make it so much easier to keep a home going.

For myself personally, enough to live on, the ability to walk after years of painful, arthritic knees. Assistance from our government and good health for my advanced age.

Ken and I are grateful for our ability to write books for Vision Colleges and for our Vision staff who work so hard for so little. And we are grateful for our board members who give time and money to help the Colleges.

Praise God for our Vision staff
who work so hard for the joy of serving
to spread the Whole Word
to the Whole World.

There are government members too that we trust to rule us well, with our Army, Navy, Airforce and Police to keep the peace and protect us from evil.

We are grateful for Judges and lawyers who enforce the law against criminals, and we must include ambulance drivers and the many dedicated firefighters we have recently needed so desperately during the terrible bushfires. There are many hundreds here for which to be grateful; some have even made the ultimate sacrifice.

We must not forget the doctors and the nurses who take care of our health and the teachers who dedicate themselves to teach our children.

Altogether these people give us a peaceful and stable country without war.

Now I begin to understand
how ungrateful I have been!

Indeed, I am beginning to realise how blessed we are. I think of those in other lands who live without clean water and electric power to make life easier. Of those displaced persons, refugees from war, in tent cities trying to keep their babies alive with inadequate water, food and medicine. It is not their fault they are there but the fault of others who carry on wars of cruel insanity.

I begin to understand how ungrateful I have been. Lord forgive me for my gross ingratitude and help me to be always aware of how blessed we are who live in this fair land of Australia. So, as the hymn writer encourages us, "Count your blessings, name them one by one and it will surprise you what the Lord has done".[7]

**Heavenly Father**, help us always to be thankful for the blessings your pour out upon us. Help us to be aware also of your unfailing love and gracious protection. Thank you for the many people you bring into our lives to bless us by showing friendship and loving kindness. Thank you for being a shelter whenever we need one and for helping us to be overcomers in our Christian life and experience. Amen

---

[7] From the hymn by Johnson Oatman Jnr. Redemption Hymnal No. 427.

# A Testimony

*He put a new song in my mouth, a hymn of praise to our God. Many will see and fear the LORD and put their trust in him* (Psalm 40:3).

I thank you O Lord that you saved my soul
and set my feet on the rock that is Christ Jesus my Lord.

You delivered me from sin and gave me victory
over depression.
You are the one who rescued me from the kingdom
of darkness,
and brought me into the kingdom of the Son you love.
In you I have redemption, the forgiveness of sins.

Thank you for the many times you have brought
healing to my body when I needed it
How merciful and kind you have been.
Now I can live in victory.

May I be a witness of your glory to my children
and grandchildren.
May all of them be blessed through
the revelation of your great love for them
and for all mankind.

**Heavenly Father,**
Give me faith for my doubt, strength for my weakness,
Joy for my sorrow and stability for my emotions.
Let me glory in your Might, filled with awe at your Majesty,
Open to your love and light, washed with your Word.
Give me songs of worship, and a heart filled with gratitude,
Giving thanks to you Father for your everlasting love.
Amen.[8]

[8] Published in *Life of Balance* 2020

# The Humble Bee

*The Son is the image of the invisible God, the firstborn over all creation. For in him all things were created: things in heaven and on earth, visible and invisible, whether thrones or powers or rulers or authorities; all things have been created through him and for him. He is before all things, and in him all things hold together* (Colossians 1:15-17).

I cannot understand how anyone can be an atheist. Consider the humble bee. The other day on Gardening Australia I heard that it takes one thousand trips to a flower before a bee can make one teaspoon of honey!

I decided to learn more about bees. These are some of the things I learned and only a fool can believe this all happens by accident.

Here is a question: "How can we know God is there if we can't see him or touch him?"

The answer from a Naturalist is, "Because of the hairs on a bee!"

> It takes one thousand trips
> to a flower before a bee can make
> one teaspoon of honey!

**Gene Stratton Porter** wrote many books to indicate the beauties of nature and the proofs of God's existence through nature. In her magnificent story, *The Keeper of the Bees,* she tells, through her character of the Little Scout, some wonderful truths about the family of bees. Here they are drawn from several pages of the lecture the Little Scout gave to the returned soldier, James Lewis Macfarlane, who was endeavouring to care for the bees.

There are 4,500 different kinds of wild bees. 100,000 plants would not live without the Worker Bees to pollinate them. The Worker Bee that carries the pollen from flower to flower has little tubes on its nose that each have five thousand smell hollows. It has six thousand eyes on each side of its head so it can see the flowers from which it wants to harvest the pollen and the nectar.

It has two stomachs, a little one more inside for itself and a way bigger stomach, more on the outside of its body to share with the hive.

Back on its abdomen every Worker Bee has four pockets to secrete wax, and every worker has got baskets on its legs to gather pollen in, besides the nectar they carry in their stomach for the hive. Every one of them has a good sharp sting that it can use if it doesn't like your scent or if it thinks you are going to hurt it or do something you shouldn't around the hive.

Every one of them has long hair for a bee and it is soft and fine and when the worker goes into a flower these hairs fill up with pollen too, as well as its baskets, and it is the law, because of God, that when any bee starts out to gather nectar and pollen it never mixes one flower with another but stays with the one with which it began. The bee does the flower's courting for it, going from male to female of the same species.

That means, if it starts on a particular flower, it keeps right on going to the same species of flower. How wonderful then is God's creation and how grateful we should be for this Worker Bee. Imagine a world with no fruit trees, no flowers, no plants that rely on the bees to pollinate them. One hundred thousand different plants would disappear altogether without the Worker Bees doing the job for which they were created.[9]

Try to imagine how many human workers would have to bend their backs for many weary hours to take the place of the bee. Even if it were possible, the cost would make food only available to the wealthy. The rest of us would soon starve.

> Imagine a world with no fruit trees, no
> flowers, no plants that rely on
> the bees to pollinate them.

God made this world and he designed it so that a large variety of food could grow during the four seasons for us to enjoy. He created the humble Worker Bee, which itself only lives for around six weeks, to make sure that plants continue to feed us.

There are many more wonderful things we could say about the bees, the Queen the nymphs and the drones, but this is enough to fill us with wonder at God's careful planning.

---

[9] Facts taken from *The Keeper of the Bees* by Gene Stratton Porter Published by Indiana University Press 1991.

How terrible it is then that we are close to losing our bees through the indiscriminate use of DDT. and the pollution we are producing by some of our modern inventions. I wonder if the famine we read about in the book of Revelation will be partly caused by the extinction of these amazing Worker Bees. It has been calculated that if the bees die then humanity will follow within four years!

A beehive is full of miracles and signs and symbols and wonders. The worker bee only lives for five or six weeks but the Queen bee lives for five or six years. When the hive gets too full the queen bee knows that she must divide the hive, so she lays a special egg and tells the workers she wants this one to be a queen. Then the workers get busy and make the royal jelly and finally a white nymph becomes a queen.

Bees make four different kinds of cells and the queen lays eggs for queens, males (drones), nurses and workers and they are each fed differently according to what the Queen decides they will be.

When the hive is full and everything is just right the Queen gathers her ladies of honour and her masons who make the combs and her workers who bring in the pollen and nectar and she takes some males and some nurses and she goes right away, leaving all she has achieved and begins again. Usually about two thirds of the hive goes with the Queen.

Meanwhile in the old nest the new Queen has been born and so the life of the hive goes on. The new queen establishes herself by first going in and out of the nest three or four times so she will know which is her hive, then she flies as high as she can, and the drones fly after her. One of the drones is the lucky one who gets to mate with the Queen. When this is accomplished the rest of the Queen eggs and the drones are all killed as they are no longer needed.

I found all of this quite fascinating and once again I cannot understand how anyone can be an atheist. They must just close their eyes to the wonders that are all around them. Puffed up with their own "wisdom" they place themselves above the Lord of Glory. I pity them.

> I found the bees fascinating and cannot understand how anyone who studies them can be an atheist.

Here is more up to date news about bees from the internet:

"There are about 20,000 different species of bees in the world. Bees live in colonies and there are three types of bees in each colony. There is the queen bee, the worker bee and the drone. The worker bees and the queen bee are female, but only the queen bee can reproduce.

"**All drones are male.** Worker bees clean the hive, collecting pollen and nectar to feed the colony and they take care of the offspring. The drone's only job is to mate with the queen if he becomes the chosen one, the one who can fly the highest and prove himself the best and strongest drone of all.

"**The queen's only job is to lay eggs**. Bees store their venom in a sac attached to their stinger and only female bees sting. That is because the stinger, called an ovipositor, is part of the female bee's reproductive design. A queen bee uses her ovipositor to lay eggs as well as sting.

"**Sterile females**, also called worker bees, don't lay eggs. They just use their ovipositors to sting. Bees see all colours except the colour red. That and their sense of smell help them find the flowers they need to collect pollen. Not only is pollen a food source for bees, but some of the pollen is dropped in flight, resulting in cross pollination. The relationship between the plant and the insect is called symbiosis.

"Certain species of bees die after stinging because their stingers, which are attached to their abdomen, have little barbs or hooks on them. When this type of bee tries to fly away after stinging something, part of the abdomen is ripped away causing death."

All in all, these are wonderful creatures and can only have been created by the hand of God.

**Heavenly Father**, how marvellous and intricate is your creation of the bee. Such a tiny, busy creature, living only a short time yet being a great blessing to our human race. Some of your creations are lovely to observe, and others give us food to sustain us. You have made provision for all your creatures, showing your great mercy and unfailing love. We are in awe of your abilities, so worthy of our praise and worship. Amen

# Overcoming

*For though we live in the world, we do not wage war as the world does. The weapons we fight with are not the weapons of the world. On the contrary, they have divine power to demolish strongholds* (2 Corinthians 10:3-4).

In the year I turned fourteen I had a serious illness which could have ended my life within twelve months. This required an operation which took several hours and while I was under the anaesthetic, I had a distinct experience of being rolled in a burning fire. When I looked up, I could see Jesus in the distance, but he had his arms folded as if he could not rescue me. Now, I had accepted Jesus when only twelve but had not progressed in the Christian life beyond that. I spoke of this experience to my mother, and she thought it might have been due to the long period of being under the diethyl ether that caused me to have this experience and not to worry about it.

However, I was not able to forget this very real vision so for the next year I sought most earnestly to progress in my Christian life and with the help of friends who prayed for me I became filled with the Holy Spirit on Easter Saturday 1949. That is now over seventy years ago, but it is as fresh in my memory as if it was yesterday. The experience of being filled with the Holy Spirit felt for me as though I had touched the reality of God and after that I can never doubt God is close and that he loves me dearly.

Three years later I met my husband Ken and in time we realized that the same Easter Saturday I was filled with the Holy Spirit he was at a Baptist Youth Camp giving his life to God for full time service. I like to imagine God was planning our future on that day though we were not to meet for a further three years. Now, we have been in full time service together for the Lord for sixty-six years and we have had many interesting and exciting adventures. After twenty-five years in pastoral ministry God enabled us to begin the Vision Colleges program in 1974 and this has touched lives all over the world. During the last forty-seven years we have had over two million graduates and over 10,000 churches have been established.[10]

Now in our old age God is still caring for us through our daughter Sharon who is a rich blessing to us both.

**Heavenly Father,** I give you praise for your care of us over the years we have served you. You have kept us through the good times and the sad times and brought us through to a place of peace and rest in you in our old age. Thank you that you are the same for all your children, always willing to hear our prayers and to answer them far more wonderfully than we can even imagine. Amen

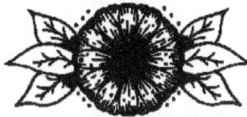

---

[10] For more information on Vision Colleges see *The History of Vision*; Vision Publishing 2014

# Comfort in Sorrow

*Praise be to the God and Father of our Lord Jesus Christ, the Father of compassion and the God of all comfort, who comforts us in all our troubles, so that we can comfort those in any trouble with the comfort we ourselves receive from God* (2 Corinthians 1:3-4)

I called out to God from
The depths of my sorrow.
He heard me from his Temple,
His grace, love and mercy to bestow.
Holding my lost little one close to his heart,
Jesus comforted me.

My babe will never know
The joy of paddling in the sea,
Or of playing happily
With friends and family.
"Neither will he suffer any pain or fear",
My Lord whispers to me softly to comfort me.

One day I'll see my babe in glory.
Though I don't know how he will appear,
One thing I know,
Jesus understands my fears,
He saw my bitter tears,
And he did not turn from me.

What I have suffered was
First suffered by him alone.
On the cross he felt all the pains
Of sickness and disease; all the groans
Of heartbreak and despair,
All were laid on him.

There, the terrible battle finished,
Jesus' loving heart was broken.
But that moment of seeming defeat
Brought victory,
A strong token of his love.
We who sorrow can rest, assured he cares.

Comfort is ours from God,
Who is all compassion and mercy.
We who sorrow can be blessed
Through understanding
Our need to receive daily from
The loving, nurturing heart of the Father.

Then we who have been comforted
Can in turn comfort others
With the comfort we have
Received from heaven.
Making parents who have lost a child aware
God's love and mercy avail in times of sorrow.[11]

---

[11] In memory of our son, Gavin James Chant, born 2nd November, died 4th November 1957.

**Heavenly Father**, thank you for being strong to deliver. Thank you for being our fortress and our strong tower. Thank you for being our shield and rampart, our dwelling place and our refuge forever. Thank you for your mercy and comfort when we are sorrowful, thank you that you give us the courage to continue our daily walk when we have suffered the death of a loved one. Help us to trust in you completely, drawing strength from the indwelling Holy Spirit who helps us to pray when we don't know how to pray. Amen.

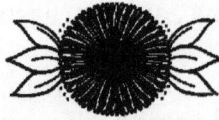

# Pilgrim's Progress

*To this you were called, because Christ suffered for you, leaving you an example, that you should follow in his steps* (1 Peter 2:21).

I have been re-reading *Pilgrim's Progress* by John Bunyan and the beginnings of his Christian walk are very similar to our own spiritual journey.

First, Christian becomes despondent. He is depressed because of his burden of sin, but he doesn't know what to do about it. So, he tries to earn his salvation by keeping the law. Then he meets Evangelist who points him in the right direction.

He finally makes it onto the Narrow Way and falls at the foot of the cross. His burden of sin rolls away and is lost forever. Then he continues on his way with joy in his heart.

We all go through a similar journey to become a Christian. We feel our burden of sin, we try to keep the law, but fail miserably. Then joy fills our heart when it is explained to us that salvation is by grace alone! All we have to do is believe and receive.

Christian had many adventures on his way to heaven in the story, and we all have our own pilgrimage to walk and our own life problems to overcome.

Ancient pilgrims who did not know the scriptures as we do made pilgrimage to many bizarre remains of saints they admired. We who have so many translations of the Bible to enjoy and the right to read them for ourselves know better!

There are three things we need to remember on our pilgrimage from earth to glory. To keep our eyes on our Saviour, Jesus, to walk in his steps as closely as we can, and to keep our eyes on the city whose builder and maker is God.

If we do these things, we will have an abundant entrance into God's kingdom and a commendation, *"Well done good and faithful servant!"*

**Heavenly Father**, thank you for the great salvation you have given us. We rejoice in this story of the Pilgrim's Progress which explains so much of the Christian life. Thank you for the author, John Bunyan, who was willing to go to prison for twelve years for preaching your Word. Thank you for giving him the idea to write the story of a Christian's journey through life which has been such a blessing to so many for more than a hundred years. Amen

# Faithfulness

*Because of the LORD'S great love we are not consumed, for his compassions never fail. They are new every morning; great is your faithfulness* (Lamentations 3:22-23).

**Peacock Iris**: In my garden I have a delicate flower. It is white with a glossy black and blue peacock eye. It blooms once a year and is similar to a day lily as each flower lasts but one full day and then by evening has closed up again. Each day during the season there are more and more flowers blooming to fill our family with delight.

These flowers that come and go so swiftly remind me of God's great love and compassion which Jeremiah tells us are renewed each morning. Fresh and dainty and prolific these flowers bloom, one after another, day after day before they finally cease flowering for another year. The leaves of this plant remain green always and quickly fill up the space provided for them by producing many more plants.

Our God is a faithful God. Even though we are many times lacking in faith, he is always there for us to turn to when we are ready to believe in his love and mercy.

**The Passion flower – Passiflora**: In my garden I also have a prolific passionfruit vine which unfortunately grows no passion fruit but does put on a lovely show of flowers which have a history.

They were named by the Spanish Jesuit missionaries who discovered them in the jungles of South America. They were amazed to note so many reminders in the flower of the passion, or suffering, of Christ. The five petals and five sepals were said to symbolise the ten original apostles who were martyred for their faith. The showy corona was said to represent either the crown of thorns or the halo of Christ.

The five stamens are said to represent the five wounds inflicted on Jesus. That is the nails through his hands and feet and the spear wound in his side. The plants climbing tendrils were said to represent the cords or scourges and the handsome palmate leaves the hands of Christ's tormentors. [12]

Thank you, Lord for this lovely flower which represents the story of your sufferings and the number of the disciples who spread your message at the risk of their lives. Thank you for the missionaries who saw the symbolism and recorded their thoughts about the flowers for us.

**Heavenly Father**, thank you, for the prophet Jeremiah and the wonderful words he wrote about your compassion which he found to be new every morning. Thank you that you care for those who are suffering. This indicates that you are always watching over us and you care when we are hurt or in trouble. You have told us that even the sparrows do not fall to the ground without you knowing it. Truly you are a God past finding out, so compassionate and kind. Help us to appreciate your love and to thank you for caring for us every day. Amen

---

[12] Information taken from *What Flower is That* by Stirling Macoboy.

# The Nautilus Shell

*For since the creation of the world God's invisible qualities - his eternal power and divine nature have been clearly seen, being understood from what has been made, so that people are without excuse* (Roman 1:20).

There are many beautiful shells that can be found on our seashores, but the Nautilus shell is by far the most fascinating to me. The precision of the swirls and the tiny compartments so neatly laid out speak to me of the creative ability of our God and his mathematical beauty. There are other colourful and beautiful shells, such as the paua shell of New Zealand, from which can be made pieces of jewellery. There are many different sizes and shapes of shells, each having a purpose for a time until the creature either outgrows or abandons its shell or dies.

God is a perfect mathematician.
We see this everywhere in nature.

While my husband and I were in the Bahamas I saw an enormous shell. It must have weighed at least ten to fifteen kilos and I wanted to buy it and take it home to Australia with me. However, Ken said, "You buy it, you carry it." I realised sadly that it was not practical with the luggage we already had to even contemplate buying the shell and attempting to take it home with us. It was truly magnificent, but I had to leave it there. I may have had trouble bringing it through customs as well and that would have been heartbreaking. To carry it all that way only to lose it in the end!

God is a perfect mathematician. We see this everywhere in nature. Take a flower and trace the petals and the stamens. How carefully they follow the precision of geometric design. The infinite variety of the flowers that we have the privilege of enjoying are amazing.

Then there are the leaves on a eucalyptus tree, and many other equally fascinating shapes and sizes of leaves on the thousands of varieties of trees that grow in this world of ours. God is a God of precision and detail and how can anyone believe that the fascinating plants in our world came about by chance or evolution. As the scripture says, if they believe our world came about through chance, without God's creative ability, *"They are without excuse."*

**Heavenly Father,** thank you, that though you are invisible to our eyes, yet we see your qualities in the natural creation all around us. We pray for those who cannot see you, or who refuse to see you, in your beautiful creation. Open their eyes Lord that they may see you before it is too late for them to trust in you for their salvation. May they break through their unbelief into a believing faith in you and in your everlasting love. We know it is not your will that any should perish but that all should come to a knowledge of the truth. Amen

# The Monarch Butterfly

*Dear friends, now we are children of God, and what we will be has not yet been made known. But we know that when Christ appears, we shall be like him, for we shall see him as he is* (1 John 3:2).

The metamorphosis of the Monarch butterfly can illustrate in some ways the mystery of our soul and spirit. The caterpillar being likened to our human body, and the creative changes going on within the chrysalis formed by the caterpillar, illustrating the soul and spirit merging into a beautiful new creation.

There is a fascination in the life cycle of the Monarch butterfly. It begins with an egg planted by the adult butterfly on a leaf of the plant it prefers. When the egg hatches it becomes a caterpillar that eats steadily and grows until, shedding and renewing its skin several times, it reaches adulthood. It then forms a chrysalis around itself which attaches to a tree branch.

God rearranges the molecules!

Inside the chrysalis, over a period of fifteen days, the elements which made up the caterpillar move around, rearranging the molecules, until a miracle occurs, and the adult butterfly emerges – a creature so beautiful and so changed from its caterpillar form that it seems impossible the two elements have come from the same origin.[13]

---

[13] A film on the metamorphosis of the Monarch Butterfly can be seen on Wikipedia.

> We know that when Christ appears, we
> shall be like him, for we shall
> see him as he is (1 John 3:2b).

One day when the Lord Jesus returns to this world, we will be caught up to meet him, transformed from this realm to an eternal life in him. Our inner new creation will be revealed; we shall be like Jesus for we will see him as he is.

**Heavenly Father**, how wonderful is your creation of the butterfly and how intricate is the metamorphosis it goes through while hidden in its chrysalis. Truly there are many mysteries in this world of ours and there are still many things we do not understand. Scientists are trying to discover life but there are some things that belong to you alone O Lord. I wonder how far you will let them proceed before you say, "Enough". Each day knowledge is increasing and with the help of computers men have come a long way toward knowing your secrets. I pray that in their lust for discovery they will not bring an end to mankind. Because of these things we look forward to your second coming Lord Jesus when you will put an end to wickedness and rule over this world with justice and wisdom. Amen

# His Love Endures Forever

*Give thanks to the LORD, for he is good. His love endures forever* (Psalm 136:1).

When you read this Psalm 136 you will note that if you remove the words, *'His Love endures forever'*, then the text reads as a testimony. I have followed that same idea here.

God is great; he is full of Majesty
His love endures forever

He rules on high; earth is his footstool
His love endures forever

He created the stars by his spoken word
His love endures forever

He knows them all by name
His love endures forever

He brings out the sun in the morning
His love endures forever

And the moon at night to give us light
His love endures forever

His eyes search throughout the earth
His love endures forever

Seeking any who will listen and obey.
His love endures forever

He looked down upon my poor estate
His love endures forever

My soul was trapped in the mire
His love endures forever

I could see no way out
His love endures forever

But the Lord saw my trouble
His love endures forever

He delivered me from the thrall of sin
His love endures forever

He rescued me from the snare of the fowler
His love endures forever

He is with me each day to encourage me
His love endures forever

He tastes like honey in the rock
His love endures forever

He is my sweet deliverer who cleanses me
His love endures forever

My high tower into whom I can run
His love endures forever

He gives me a fresh start each day
His love endures forever

I will praise him always
His love endures forever

No matter when trials come
His love endures forever

I trust in him completely
His love endures forever

His faithfulness is new every morning
His love endures forever

And he keeps his promises
His love endures forever

Praise and worship belong to him
His love endures forever.

**Heavenly Father**, thank you, that your love is unfailing, everlasting, enduring forever, faithful, righteous, wonderful, precious, compassionate and true. There is no shadow of turning with you. You do not change, and we know we can trust you to care for us and protect us forever. Thank you for your great love. Amen

# The Diary of a Daffodil
### An Imaginative Meditation

*See how the flowers of the field grow. They do not labour or spin. Yet I tell you that not even Solomon in all his splendour was dressed like one of these.* (Matthew 6:28b-29).

I began as a small ugly shape and was tortured for many weeks by extreme cold. Now I have been given a warm snug bed of soil and I can feel the warm yellow sun drawing me upward toward the light.

Life is pulsating through me, my roots are reaching down absorbing nourishment and slowly I am palpitating, pushing and peering up into the air. Yes, I have pierced through the last barriers and have been able to look around me at last. What exquisite relief! I am planted by a stream and as far as I can see there are others, like myself, all around me.

Today, I feel different. I have grown a protuberance. I am filled with excitement! Soon I will know the answer to the mystery of life. What am I? What will I look like when I am fully grown?

Many days pass as I sway in the light of the warm yellow sun, and many a night finds me cooling in the lighter rays of the moon and stars so far above me. The regular intervals of warmth and cold bring a rhythm that settles over me like music. A breeze sways my brothers and sisters, and we touch briefly and bow to one another again and again.

> Many a night finds me cooling
> in the lighter rays of the moon.

At last! I am revealed as a cream and yellow beauty, one of many others, bursting forth into acres of rich yellow, trumpet like blooms. We are daffodils! How exquisite we are. We sway and dip with the sweet zephyrs that dance here and there among us while the constant ripples of the stream below make beautiful reflective patterns to delight the eye.

I shiver with joy, for we are to become famous! Today a man named Wordsworth came to see us, he sat among us, and we heard him speak. At first, he sounded depressed and lonely but soon his voice grew stronger until it rang with triumph. Yes, though we must soon fade and die we will yet be immortal, no one will be able to forget our yellow beauty. Listen, he still speaks...

> I wandered lonely as a cloud
> That floats on high o'er vales and hills,
> When all at once I saw a crowd,
> A host, of golden daffodils.
> Beside the lake, beneath the trees,
> Fluttering and dancing in the breeze.
>
> Continuous as the stars that shine
> And twinkle on the milky way,
> They stretched in never ending line
> Along the margin of a bay:
> Ten thousand saw I at a glance
> Tossing their heads in sprightly dance.[14]

---

[14] *I Wandered Lonely as A Cloud* by W. Wordsworth; The first two Stanzas from The Pageant of English Poetry, Page 545.

**Heavenly Father**, thank you for a sense of humour and the ability to enjoy life and happiness. Thank you for the poets who have written about the mountains, the valleys, the forests and the flowers in all your great creation. Thank you for the daffodils and for all the beautiful flowers you have created for us to enjoy. In them we see but a shadow of your greater beauty and glory. We know heaven is real and this world but a poor copy and so we thank you that one day we will see heaven's beauty and enjoy it with our loved ones who have gone before us. Amen

# A Meditation on Friendship

*Do two walk together unless they have agreed to do so?* (Amos 3:3).

We have a quote on our bedroom wall, a quote on friendship from the busy author, James Boswell, who wrote the life of Samuel Johnson, the editor of the best and most comprehensive English dictionary of the era. I wonder if Boswell was thinking of his friend Johnson when he wrote it?

"We cannot tell the precise moment when friendship is formed. It is in filling a vessel drop by drop there is at last a drop which makes it run over. So, in a series of kindnesses there is at last one which makes the heart run over"

When making friendships, be careful to avoid those who say they are your friends but are in reality quite selfish in their demands. Evade also, those you can discern are immoral, lazy, angry or covetous. Most important of all, beware of those who may be of good character, but who do not believe in God or in his Son, Jesus. Avoid them all, for darkness overcomes light unless we are careful to maintain our Christian testimony.

The right kind of friends are those who help us grow and develop mentally by challenging our wrong thinking, and then help us to grow spiritually through their conversation and prayers. These friends will support us when we are anxious or depressed and help us to renew our mind by encouraging us to read the Word of God and study it regularly.

**The rules of friendship.**

Show an interest in others. Don't focus on your own troubles. Accept people unconditionally; be a good listener. Sympathise when it is needed and try to understand the problem your friend is suffering if there is one. People need to feel they are significant and that you care about them. But don't give up on your friends even when the going is tough; share your testimony with them. Tell them how Jesus helps you to overcome your problems and to make good decisions.

**Love is a verb.**

Love is not emotion – when love is present there may be an emotional response, but this in itself is not love.

Love is not pity. Those who love will feel pity, but pity can be felt without love. Pity feels sorrow and shakes its head, love moves in to help. Love is a doing word!

True love is unconditional!

True love is unconditional. It needs the same quality of freedom that God's love expresses. That is, freedom to be yourself, to make your own decisions, and to live your own life.

Human love is often only selfishness pretending to be love. If, what we call love smothers another person, or forces control over them, or if it is proud and refuses to let the other person be an individual with thoughts and preferences of their own, then it is not real love.

Unconditional love has this to say,

"I love you for yourself, not for what you can give me or for what you are able to be or do. Just as you are, faults and all."[15]

**Heavenly Father**, thank you for your great love and for the fact that it is unconditional. You loved us before we loved you. You drew us to you by your great love and we feel safe and secure in that love. Help us to love and serve others just as they are without expecting anything in return. May we give those we love the freedom to be themselves and to follow their own path and help us to remember to treat others as we would like them to treat us. Amen

[15] Unfortunately, I have lost the source of this quote.

# Falling in Love

*Love is patient, love is kind. It does not envy, it does not boast, it is not proud. It does not dishonour others, it is not self-seeking, it is not easily angered, it keeps no record of wrongs. Love does not delight in evil but rejoices with the truth. It always protects, always trusts, always hopes, always perseveres. Love never fails* (1 Corinthians 13:4-8a).

Young people mistake 'lust' for 'love'. Lust is merely a chemical reaction between two people that dies when that lust is satisfied. True love shares the same chemical reaction, but it is curtailed and denied until friendship and mutuality are explored and established. This discipline lays a firm foundation for a lifetime together in marriage.

Because young people are ignorant of this truth, they mistake lust for love and when that excitement dies away, if they have not built a lasting friendship, they have nothing left on which to build their marriage.

Instead of teaching the physical aspects of sex in schools it would be far better to teach young people on how to build good relationships, and lasting friendships. Keeping the mutuality of race, culture, creed, and education in mind.

We should teach young people
how to build good relationships.

Though it is not impossible for a couple to make a good marriage if they do not have complete mutuality, they will have to work harder at understanding one another. Very importantly, there will have to be a mutual agreement on how to raise any children of the union.

**Heavenly Father,** thank you for friendship and for loving family life. I pray for those who don't have happiness in their family. For those who suffer harm, for the women and children who are battered and bruised. This is the work of the enemy, and these families need to acknowledge Jesus as Saviour and then to be taught how to live, how to forgive and how to love each other sincerely. Lord, if possible, I pray you will provide teachers who will go into the high schools and teach young people how to live and love in a godly manner. I pray for those who suffer from mental illness and pray for places where these people can be prayed for and helped to gain victory over depression and anxiety. Amen

# Bumble Bee Biscuits

*And the God of all grace, who called you to his eternal glory in Christ, after you have suffered a little while, will himself restore you and make you strong firm and steadfast* (1 Peter 5:10).

I received a recipe from a friend in New Zealand, a biscuit of hers I had enjoyed. It involved crushing plain sweet biscuits and then adding some other ingredients such as dried fruit and condensed milk and coconut. There was no cooking involved so I thought it would be a simple and tasty, sweet, for my children. While I was crushing the biscuits, I pondered within myself.

"What would these biscuits say to me if they could talk?"

Then I thought it likely they would say, "What are you doing to me? Why are you crushing me?"

What would be my answer? I think my answer would be, "I am crushing you to make something better and more wonderful from you."

After completing these thoughts, straight away I saw the connection with Christians and the way the Lord trains us for service. A recipe for God's discipline!

What do we say to the Lord when we are going through a tough time? Usually it is, "Why is this happening to me?"

How does the Lord answer us? I think his answer would be something like this:

"Whatever is behind any experience, or whatever causes it, is not important. Each experience, even though it may be hard and stressful while you are going through it, can make you into someone with a finer and deeper character. If you keep a right attitude, then each experience can enrich you and make you more useful for the Kingdom of God."

A fanciful image? Or, as I would rather think, a nudge from the Holy Spirit to teach me, through the simple homely task of preparing Bumble Bee biscuits for my children, that God is always interested in everything we do and uses every experience to further his plans for us.

**Heavenly Father**, I thank you that you speak to us with the still small voice of the Holy Spirit and that there is nothing in our life too small or insignificant for you to make use of, to teach us of your ways. Help us to be aware at all times of everyday lessons you want us to learn. Help us to take notice of your discipline and to be obedient to your instructions. Amen

# God's Care

*Whoever dwells in the shelter of the Most-High will rest in the shadow of the Almighty* (Psalm 91:1).

In this incredible Psalm 91 we are given picture after picture depicting the caring love of our God.

The first picture is of God's shadow and the idea is that on a hot and weary day, when the battle seems too overwhelming for us to endure, we can rest in the shadow of God's sheltering throne where we can find refreshing coolness from the heat of the day.

In the 91st Psalm we are given pictures of the caring love of God.

The second picture is of a strong and mighty fortress with battlements and narrow windows to keep out the arrows of our enemies. In this fortress we can feel safe and sure, surrounded completely by our Almighty God whom we can trust to keep us safe.

The third picture is of a broody hen spreading her wings to keep her chickens safe from harm. Surely our God is such a shelter, and we are reminded of the words of Jesus on his way into Jerusalem for the Passover and his ultimate death on the cross.

*"Jerusalem, Jerusalem, you who kill the prophets and stone those sent to you, how often I have longed to gather your children together, as a hen gathers her chicks under her wings, and you were not willing* (Matthew 23:37).

The fourth picture is of God's faithfulness as a shield and rampart. The shields in the Old Testament days were very large and tall, covering the whole body of the soldier and keeping him safe from the swords and arrows of his enemies. A rampart was a wall built to keep out the enemy so these two are a good depiction of God's faithful love keeping us safe from our enemies while we fight with the Word and prayer to overcome them.

Sometimes, it is possible God saves us from harm of which we are unaware. If our eyes were opened to the spiritual realm, we might be astonished at the many times God sends his angels to keep us safe.

The fifth picture is of the Lord as a dwelling place, a refuge from the battle. A place where we can rest and be at peace while we refuel for future battles. We are promised that if we make God our refuge then he will command his angels to guard us in all our ways.

The last part of this wonderful psalm is in the form of prophecy. It is God speaking. He says that because we love him and acknowledge him, he will rescue us, protect us, be with us in trouble, honour us, satisfy us with long life and show us his salvation.

**Heavenly Father,** thank you for all the pictures you give us in this psalm of your loving care. Help us to have faith in you and to trust in you without fail. Thank you for making provision to keep us safe from the enemy and to bring us safely into your presence at last. Grant us the courage we need to complete the assignments you have given us. Thank you for the wisdom and faithfulness to finish our works of service, and the health and strength to bring them to completion. Amen

# The Word of God

*Blessed are those whose ways are blameless, who walk according to the law of the Lord* (Psalm 119:1).

There is blessing and honour in obeying the Word of God and we should be steadfast in keeping it. If we consider the Word and meditate on it constantly then it will keep us on the right path. If we hide it in our heart, it will keep us from sin. We can ask God to teach us his way and speaking his Word aloud will bring us great joy.

We must not neglect God's Word but ask him to open our eyes and give us revelation concerning it. I know God will rebuke me if I stray from his Word, but he will be gracious to me also and broaden my understanding because of his faithfulness. I trust him to turn my eyes away from worthless things toward such things as love, trust, freedom, delight, comfort, preservation and songs in the night.

Suffering is good for me. Lord, you created me, and you are faithful to discipline me when necessary. Your Word is precious to me, and your compassion gives me life. I will wholeheartedly follow your Word. Persecution won't keep me from your Word because your words are sweet to my taste, a lamp and a light I can follow. They are the willing praise of my mouth and the joy of my heart, my heritage.

It is you, Lord, who are my refuge and my shield, my hope is in your Word. You sustain me, uphold me and deliver me. I stand in awe of your Word. Give me discernment so I can understand it always because I love your commands more than gold. Direct my footsteps according to your Word and let no sin rule over me. Your promises have been thoroughly tested and I love them. May my lips overflow with praise and may my tongue sing of your Word for all your commands are righteous.

The Law is my schoolmaster to bring me to Christ and thus to eternal life. God's statutes are trustworthy. They are the building blocks of his Kingdom. His precepts are right. They show us how to live. His commands are radiant. They keep us in his will. Our fear and respect for God, keep us from careless living. His ordinances are sure. They keep us steady in our Christian life.

He revives our soul, he makes us wiser than we are, our heart overflows with joy as we understand his Word. We respect our Lord and want to please him in all things.

Altogether, God's government is more precious than gold and sweeter than honey. If we are obedient to the Lord, we will never lack any good thing. Instead, we will successfully complete our life journey, accomplishing for God all that he planned for us before we were born.[16]

**Heavenly Father**, we thank you for your everlasting Word and the instruction it gives to us in how to live in a way that pleases you. We know that if we keep your Word, we will have great success in the life you planned for us before we were born, and that we will not lack any good thing from your hand. Help us always to take heed to your scriptures and study them well because they will be a light to our path and give strength to our witness. Amen

---

[16] In Psalm 119 king David shows us these many ways to describe the Law of the Lord.

# Meditations from Galatians

(Taken from the translation of the Message Bible).

Thank you, Jesus, for rescuing us from this evil world system by offering yourself as a sacrifice for our sins.

Thank you for choosing us before we were even born.

Thank you for revealing yourself to us who believe.

Thank you that because we believed in you as the Messiah we are set right before God. By trusting in you, not by trying to be good.

Thank you that the life I live is not 'mine', but it is lived by faith in you, Jesus, who loved me and gave yourself for me and for all who believe.

Thank you that those who live by faith are blessed along with Abraham, because anyone who tries to live by his own effort independent of God is doomed to failure.

Thank you that you redeemed us from a self- defeating, cursed life by absorbing it completely into yourself.

Thank you that you dissolved the curse of sin and now we are able to receive God's life, his Holy Spirit, by believing.

Thank you that in your family there is neither Jew, nor gentile, slave nor free, male nor female. In Christ all are equal.

Thank you that we are heirs of the promises, that we are fully adopted into your family.

Thank you that we are heirs with complete access to the inheritance of the saints.

Thank you that you set us free to live a life of freedom.

Thank you that we can use this freedom to serve one another in love.

Thank you for the fruits of the Spirit you develop in us: -

Affection for others (love).

Exuberance about life (joy).

Serenity (peace).

Through your Spirit we develop a willingness to stick with things (patience).

A sense of compassion in the heart (kindness).

And a conviction that a basic holiness pervades things and people (goodness).

We find ourselves involved in loyal commitments (fidelity).

Not needing to force our way in life (gentleness).

Able to marshal and direct our energies wisely (self-control).

Thank you for teaching us that we should bear one another's burdens. And for warning us that we will reap what we sow.

**Heavenly Father**, how pleasant it is to trust in your Word and to have faith in your great love. Thank you for the fruit of the Spirit through which the Holy Spirit produces the character of Christ in us. Help us to bear the burdens and share the troubles of those close to us and so fulfill the love of Christ. May we always remember, we reap what we sow, and that if we sow your precious Word into our life, we will reap a good harvest. Amen

# Seeds

*Then God said, "Let the land produce vegetation: seed-bearing plants and trees on the land that bear fruit with seed in it, according to their various kinds." And it was so* (Genesis 1: 11).

There are very many seeds in this world of ours. Some large, others small, some minute. But each seed produces after its kind. If someone were to gather seeds of various plants and place them before you, would you be able to tell what fruit would come from each of the seeds offered?

Some are familiar, and from them it is easy to name the plant that would grow if it was planted. The mango seed for instance is rather large and easily remembered if you have ever eaten a mango. Apple seeds and others with which we are familiar would also be readily named, but unless you are a keen gardener there are many seeds that would be a puzzle to you.

Take the seeds of the orange and lemon trees, they are very similar, and it would be almost impossible to work out which of these two seeds would produce the orange or the lemon tree.

Some seeds are large and some similar in size to grains of sand. Only an expert gardener is able to sort out the various seeds into their categories. Thankfully, we amateur gardeners are able to buy seeds in packets with instructions on how to plant and then care for the fruit or vegetable pictured.

The amazing wonder remains
that everything each seed needs
to complete its task is right there within it!

The amazing wonder remains that everything each seed needs to complete its task is right there within it. Only Almighty God could place in each seed the complex instructions needed for its successful future life.

First, each seed must die and then be reborn; it must almost disappear before the new shoot struggles to the surface. Only God can place what amounts to a computer of instructions into every seed, no matter how tiny.

Another thing amazes me. The prolific way in which God arranges for the multiplication of each seed.

We can count how many seeds in an apple but only God knows how many apples will be produced from one of those seeds. One apple seed could produce an apple tree and there would be many apples grown on that tree. In turn these would have the potential to produce thousands, perhaps millions of apples, into the future.

Of the divine presence within creation, Chesterton writes in "The Holy of Holies".

Speller of the stones and weeds,
Skilled in nature's crafts and creeds,
Tell me what is in the heart
Of the smallest seeds.

God Almighty, and with Him
Cherubim and Seraphim,
Filling all eternity –
Adonai Elohim.[17]

Truly our wonderful God has made it possible for us to feed even the billions of people we now have on this planet. Though, through evil wars and consequent displacement of persons there is hunger and even famine in some countries.

With climate change too, their remains an uncertain future for the human race with forest fires, floods, tornadoes and hurricanes increasing in severity. Couple these with plagues of locusts and the spectre of famine for all looms on the horizon.

Currently food is wasted by First World Countries and they will be judged by God if they do not share with other nations who remain in desperate need.

I have vivid memories of the war years 1939-1945 when food was scarce, and we needed ration books as well as money to buy groceries. The ration books were divided up into small squares and the various items being purchased were worth certain numbers of squares.

---

[17] Christian History Magazine Vol xx1 No. 3 – Stanza from *The Holy of Holies* by G. K. Chesterton, Page 24.

These squares were removed by the grocer, depending on what we ordered. In this way food was equally divided between families and there was no waste. This idea may return if food becomes scarce again.

**Heavenly Father**, we know that in the end times there will be pestilence and famine and these days seem to grow ever closer. We pray for wisdom during days of pandemic with Covid-19. We need much wisdom, and good common sense, to discover what we need to do to gain the best outcome for our family and our church family. May we always have sufficient to feed our loved ones and any others who are in need. We know you are a miracle working God and that you see way into the future. Show us what we need to do to keep safe in these dark days. Amen

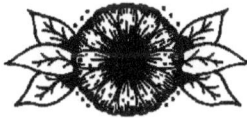

# God Has Secrets

*But about that day or hour no one knows, not even the angels in heaven, nor the Son, but only the Father* (Matthew 24:36)

*Of a truth it is, that your God is a God of gods, and a Lord of kings, and a revealer of secrets, seeing thou couldest reveal this secret* (Daniel 2:47 KJV).

God planted secrets in the sea, beautiful shells and myriad sea creatures. He stored secrets in the ground when he laid down the coal and the oil we would need for energy long before we discovered such things. He also prepared precious stones, diamonds, rubies, emeralds, sapphires and other semi-precious stones to delight us.

**God has a secret place.**

*"He who dwells in the secret place will abide under the shadow of the Almighty"* (Psalm 91:1 KJV). Whoever goes to the Lord for safety, whoever remains under the protection of the Almighty, can say to him, "You are my defender and protector, my refuge and my fortress."

**God had a secret plan**.

Jesus was God's first secret plan to bring us salvation. He came to reveal God's Kingdom and to become the High King of the Kingdom until all things are fulfilled. Jesus laid down the manifesto of his Kingdom for us, and we find it in the gospel of Matthew. We should learn his rules by heart to help us live right.

**God had another secret plan.**

This was for everyone to be included in the salvation God had prepared. No one was to miss out, all were to be invited. Not just God's special people – the Jews - but everyone in the whole world. Whoever comes to the cross of Jesus for cleansing from sin, no matter what their nationality, will be given a place in the Kingdom of God

**God's last precious secret.**

This is God's secret and Jesus told us that no one else knows the exact day of his return; not the angels, not the Son, only the Father (Matthew 24:36). Certainly, there are many signs pointing to that wonderful day, but many have tried and failed to make a date for the return of Christ. We must wait patiently, keeping ourselves ready for the day when the world will be put back into order and peace will reign.

**Heavenly Father**, how pleasant it is to dwell in your presence and to safely trust in you each day. We thank you for the promise of the Second Coming of Jesus with his mighty angels. We look forward to that great day with excitement and anticipation. What a wonder it will be to see those who have died trusting in Jesus rising again from their graves. Only you Father, know when that day and that hour will come, and we are content to leave that in your hands. But help us always to be ready for that great day Lord, with plenty of the oil of your Holy Spirit within us. Amen

# Our Christmas Tree

*Now the Lord is the Spirit, and where the Spirit if the Lord is, there is freedom. And we all, who with unveiled faces contemplate the Lord's glory, are being transformed into his image with ever increasing glory, which comes from the Lord, who is the Spirit* (2 Corinthians 3:17-18).

Many years ago, we decided as a family that we were tired of artificial Christmas trees and so we shopped around for a live tree and found a Norfolk pine about three feet tall set in a garden pot. It was small but it was nice to have a real tree and we enjoyed decorating it with all our favourite Christmas decorations.

After using this tree for a few years, we grew tired of it and looked for a new idea for Christmas. What to do with our pine tree? We decided to plant it in the backyard of our home in Launceston Tasmania. What we did not realise at the time was that the tree had remained small because the pot was small. To our amazement our small tree became a giant, growing to a height of twenty-five feet within a few years. This Norfolk pine tree took over our back yard.

We sold the house some years later, so I don't know the fate of our tree. Perhaps it is still there, but more likely it has become firewood, for it would be hard to have a proper garden with a Norfolk pine taking up all the room, casting its mighty shadow over the yard and taking up all the nutrients available.

## What lesson can we learn from this memory?

When a person is set free from confinement they can grow and expand wonderfully. Whether that confinement is caused by ignorance, by sin, by wrong decisions, by drug addiction, or any other confining habit. Jesus can break the pot of sin that stops us from growing in Christ. Indeed, when Jesus comes into our life the tempter's power is broken and we are set free to grow in the family of God.

Then we find there is no limit to the expansion of our spirit as we study the Word and develop a relationship with God. As Christians the Holy Spirit of God indwells us and where the Spirit of the Lord is there is freedom! Wonderful freedom to grow and expand in the Lord so we can accomplish all he planned for us before the foundation of this world in which we live.

**Heavenly Father**, thank you, for the great freedom we have in Christ Jesus. For the freedom to grow and develop into the person you want us to be. We know you want the best for us and that everything we go through, each experience we have, takes us further into an exciting future with you. Help us to be aware at all times of your guiding hand and your still small voice. We know that if you are leading us, we will not lose our way. Thank you for your promise to be with us always, even to the end of the age. Amen

# Health and Renewal

*(God) satisfies your desires with good things so that your youth is renewed like the eagles* (Psalm 103:5).

How wonderful it is that our heavenly Father has promised us renewal of health as we put our trust in him, both in our body and in our spirit. The Lord gives strength to the weary and increases the power of the weak, indeed we will run and not grow weary, we will walk and not faint, because our hope is in him.

Dr. Don Colbert of the USA tells us how God programs the animals: "When an animal is injured or sick, what does it do? It finds a resting place where it can lap up water, and it quits eating while it heals. This is natural, instinctual wisdom that God placed within the animal kingdom."

A bird is an animal with feathers and God has programmed the eagle to rejuvenate.

If we followed the wisdom of the animal kingdom we would get better more quickly from the common cold and the more dangerous influenza. These develop when our body is trying to throw off poisonous sprays, such as DDT, that we may have imbibed from modern farming methods. Also, we can suffer illness from the fallout due to the many marvellous inventions of this century. It is wonderful to have modern conveniences, but we do pay a price for them.

I praise God for his healing and delivering power. He has healed me and also members of my family many times. Though not always, as I made clear in my book, *Divine Healing, the Wonder and the Mystery*. I can testify that he is a healing God.

Because God mentions the renewal of the eagle in the book of Isaiah, I have found it fascinating to learn how an eagle goes through its stages of restoration. This does not come about quickly or easily. Author Col Stringer gives us a unique description of the eagle's renewal.

"High in the mountains, the eagle proceeds to go through a remarkable process of rejuvenation. Firstly, it starts to pluck at some of its wing feathers. One by one the faulty feathers are 'cast out'...

"While awaiting the regrowth of its flight feathers, the eagle does something about a dull beak – perhaps blunted by rocks or the growth of calcium build up. The beak is an all-important weapon and must be kept lethally sharp. Like a soldier preparing his sword for battle, the calcifications are painstakingly ground away by the slow but steady action of the beak against the rock.

"Likewise, the talons too may be sharpened or removed altogether. Relentlessly the beak and talons are honed back to lethal sharpness, ready for the world. Eventually after many days of preening, plucking, honing, grinding and washing, the eagle is ready to return to the outside world. It spreads its huge wings and alights from the mountain peaks, a new bird. Its youth has been renewed."[18]

[18] Quote from *All About Eagles* by Col Stringer; Pub. Col Stringer Ministries Queensland Australia.

**Heavenly Father**, thank you, for your healing power, and that you are willing to heal anyone who puts their trust in you. You are a healing God and when sinners see your healing power, they are quick to acknowledge you as the only true God. We pray your healing power will be manifest more and more. We see it being displayed in other countries, but we need to see miracles of healing right here in our own land of Australia. We pray for this to happen soon as it will bring revival and then many will accept Jesus and the salvation he offers. Amen

# God as The Gardener

*Jesus said, Do not hold onto me, for I have not yet ascended to the Father* (John 20:17a).

The tender moment when Jesus revealed himself to Mary Magdalene in the garden on resurrection morning moves me deeply. Here Jesus paused in his most important journey, to ascend to his Father and complete his act of salvation for the human race. At this critical time, he was moved by Mary's weeping enough to wait a moment to comfort her. As with Mary, this is how much he loves us all, he is always waiting to comfort, heal and deliver his people when they need him.

G. K. Chesterton has an interesting slant on this most wonderful resurrection morning.

"On the third day the friends of Christ coming at daybreak to the place found the grave empty and the stone rolled away. In varying ways, they realized the new wonder; but even they hardly realized that the world had died in the night. What they were looking at was the first day of a new creation, with a new heaven and a new earth; And in the semblance of the gardener God walked again in the garden, in the cool, not of the evening but of the dawn."[19]

Isaiah 61:3b depicts the garden of God and the beautiful trees pictured there symbolize saints in the body of Christ. *"They will be called oaks of righteousness, a planting of the LORD for the display of his splendour."*

Jesus refers to his Father as the gardener also in John 15:1. *"I am the true vine, and my father is the gardener."*

---

[19] Christian History Magazine Vol xx1 No. 3; Page 30.

At the dawn of creation God made a beautiful garden in Eden and walked and talked with Adam and Eve there. After their sin and expulsion from Eden, and the subsequent history of our fallen human race, God must be looking forward to walking with his redeemed saints in his heavenly garden.

We read something about this garden in Revelation. *"On each side of the river stood the tree of life, bearing twelve crops of fruit, yielding its fruit every month. And the leaves of the tree are for the healing of the nations "*(Revelation 22:2).

**Heavenly Father**, thank you that you are the Gardener who takes care of our spiritual growth and development. May we always be willing to be pruned and disciplined by you when we need it. Thank you that we can rest in you and soak up the blessings you pour out upon us. Thank you that we do not have to try to be good but simply rest in your unchanging grace. This sets us free from the burden of sin as we live now by your Holy Spirit within us. How kind you are to provide all the grace and mercy we need. Amen

# The Promise of Peace

*Peace I leave with you; my peace I give you. I do not give to you as the world gives. Do not let your hearts be troubled and do not be afraid* (John 14:27).

This is a wonderful word, given by Jesus to his disciples who were facing separation from their beloved teacher and an uncertain future. It brings to mind green fields, thick forests and beautiful gardens. Places where one can be at rest and relax.

Jesus promises the disciples the Holy Spirit and along with him he **promises** peace, a fruit of the Spirit. Not just an ordinary emotion, but a deep abiding peace that passes all understanding. A peace that calms our fears and anxieties and brings us into a new place of understanding the deep love and care of our God. Here we rest in his mercy and grace; he is our peace. Now we can cease all personal effort to bring about our own righteousness. Instead, we can rest in the righteousness given to us by God in response to our believing faith.

He **leaves** us with his peace. It is not an emotion which comes and goes. He leaves it with us, it is a permanent peace. It abides with us continually so we can remain serene through every circumstance of life. Through the hardest times we can trust in his unfailing love to keep us safe.

He **gives** us his peace, it is a gift, all we must do is trust in him completely and rest in his unchanging love, grace and mercy. He does not give as the world gives. The peace the world gives does not last, any negative circumstance can shatter that peace, but nothing can disturb the peace Jesus gives. His peace abides!

Recently I saw a lovely quote concerning the peace of God on the internet. Here it is:

"Shalom" means more than "peace". It means, "nothing missing, nothing broken, completeness, safety, well-being, prosperity, tranquillity, perfectness, fullness and <u>no</u> deficiency".

**Heavenly Father**, thank you for the peace you have given to us. Peace that passes all understanding, and that keeps our hearts and minds tranquil. It drives out any anxiety or depression that may seek to overcome us. We rest content in your great mercy and grace and thankyou again for your peace. Amen

# Jesus The Creator

*Lift your eyes and look to the heavens. Who created all these? He who brings out the starry host one by one and calls each of them by name. Because of his great power and mighty strength, not one of them is missing* (Isaiah 40:26).

Jesus is the all-powerful and artistic creator. He created the heavens, but also the beauties of the earth and the animal kingdom such as the dimpled hand of a tiny baby or the complexity of the human eye. Some things Jesus created for their beauty, colourful flowers and trees, mountains and lakes and the surging sea. Some he created for more practical reasons, plants and animals for food for his living creatures. Others, I am convinced he created because he has a sense of humour.

Think of the platypus with its duck bill, its webbed feet, and its coat like a beaver. It swims, lays eggs, and suckles its young! What a puzzle this discovery caused for the scientists in the early days of British settlement in Australia.

Then there is the Arabian camel with its one hump which stores enough water for three to six days. It looks an ungainly figure of fun, but it can go a long time without food and its broad feet are ideal for the sandy desert. If it is set free to roam it can find its way to water through trackless desert. How wonderful are the ways of the Lord who created this humorous looking animal, perfect for the dry and sandy desert wastes.

These two comical creatures, the platypus and the camel, were created for their environment and fit perfectly into God's creation. Two of the thousands of creatures God has put into our world for our use or enjoyment.

Jesus created these things just by speaking the word and he has also given mankind the ability to create. If we have the talent, we can create art and sculpture; write books and poetry; or build architectural masterpieces.

We can also create emotions by the words we speak. We can create happiness or sadness with our words. We can uplift someone or drag them down. We can speak truth or falsehood; we can speak life or death. James warns us about the power of the tongue. *"Likewise, the tongue is a small part of the body, but it makes great boasts. Consider what a great forest is set on fire by a small spark."* (James 3:5).

**Heavenly Father**, how great is your creative genius. The universe displays your splendour, and the stars speak of your vast ability. The sun rises each morning at your decree and sets each evening to give us rest and refreshing during the night. The moon sails serenely in the sky and its presence controls the tides of our seas each day. You have arranged and created all these wonders for our benefit, and we thank you and appreciate your loving kindness Lord. Help us to always speak blessing with our words. Amen

# Meditation on Philippians

We thank you Lord Jesus
For being willing to put aside your divinity
For becoming human to die on the cross for us.

We thank you Lord Jesus
For being obedient unto death.

We thank you Lord Jesus
that you are now exalted to the highest place,
and you have a name that is above every name.

Thank you that one day every person will kneel
and acknowledge you King of kings and Lord of lords.

We thank you Lord Jesus
For your triumphant resurrection.
Thank you that you led captivity captive
And gave gifts unto men.

We thank you Lord Jesus
That you are seated in glory
at the Father's right hand
And that you are interceding for us today.

We thank you Lord Jesus
That one day we will be with you forever.
For all these things we thank you Lord Jesus
Amen.

**Heavenly Father**, we thank you for the book of Philippians and for the great teaching the apostle Paul has given to us here. This is a book of rejoicing and we do rejoice and are glad because of your eternal love for us. You have told us we must work out our salvation with fear and trembling and then you will do your part to work your good purpose in our lives. We trust you to give us tasks that we can accomplish for you with your help. Amen

# Death Where Is Your Sting?

*Precious in the sight of the LORD is the death of his faithful servants* (Psalm 116:15).

I wonder, what it is it like to die? I like to think dying is similar to being born into this world. As babies we go from a dark place of warmth and security through a painful tunnel into a bright light and a new form of existence. A place where we are surrounded by tender loving care.

I once had a moment of an out of body experience when I was birthing my daughter Sharon. All I remember is experiencing a rushing up through the air and a feeling of incredible lightness as I was separated from the weight of my earthly body.

Of course, I did not die as I was in the care of a specialist doctor who was taking good care of me. I have never forgotten the experience though, as it was so exciting and unusual.

I remember the explanation of dying given by a medical doctor to one of his patients who was afraid of death. His story involved his pet dog who was waiting for him in another room. When he called his dog and opened the door for him the dog bounded in happily, greeting his master with great exuberance. The doctor explained this is what death should be like. A moment of racing happily into the arms of our Master, Jesus, when he opens the door for us.

There is a beautiful prophecy concerning Jesus the Messiah, who was to come, in the book of Isaiah.

*On this mountain he will destroy the shroud that enfolds all peoples, the sheet that covers all nations; he will swallow up death forever. The Sovereign Lord will wipe away the tears from all faces; he will remove his peoples disgrace from all the earth. The Lord has spoken* (Isaiah 25:7-8).

In Psalm 116 we are told that our death is a precious moment for the Lord, and I suppose this is because he will be so glad that we can see him at last; that our eyes are opened to the heavenly realms. In that moment we will have no more need for faith. Seeing is believing. Remember, Jesus said to Thomas, *"Because you have seen me, you have believed; blessed are those who have not seen and yet have believed"* (John 20:29).

We are among those who have not yet seen but have believed and so there will be a special blessing for us, promised by Jesus.

**Heavenly Father**, thank you that one day you will take us to be with you forever. Death has no terrors for those who trust in you. We look forward to seeing you face to face. Help us to be ready to go to be with you when the time comes. Amen

# Meditation on Ephesians

We praise you Lord Jesus for spiritual blessings
in heavenly places.
For adopting us as your sons and daughters.
Thank you for redeeming us by your blood
And for forgiving our sins.

Thank you for making known to us
the mystery of your will,
and for choosing us before we knew you.
Thank you for Holy Spirit baptism
the guarantee of our inheritance
and for the spirit of wisdom.

Thank you, Lord Jesus, for giving us revelation
to know you better.
For opening our eyes to know
the hope you have given us,
And for your mighty strength and resurrection power.

We praise you, Lord Jesus, for you are seated far above all
rule and authority.
God has placed you head over everything.
You are head over the church, which is your body,
for God has placed everything under your feet.

Thank you, Lord Jesus, for being so rich in mercy,
and for making us alive in Christ.
Thank you for making us your handiwork,
created to do good works.

Thank you for making us fellow citizens
with God's people.
Thank you for building us on a sure foundation
where you are the cornerstone.

Thank you for giving us the power of prayer and
for being able to do more in answering us
than we can possibly imagine.

Thank you for helping us to walk
in the way of love,
and to walk as children of light.
Thank you for helping us find out what pleases you.

Thank you for teaching us to sing
psalms and hymns and songs of the Spirit.
Thank you for teaching us to give thanks to God the Father
for everything, in your name.

Thank you for teaching us to be strong in you
and to put on the full armour you have granted us.
Thank you for showing us how to pray in the Spirit,
to always be alert and speak boldly about you
and the good news of the gospel

For all these things we thank you Lord Jesus. Amen

**Heavenly Father**, thank you for the revelation in this wonderful letter. It gives us teaching on how to live for you, how to pray to you and how to please you, both in our family life and in our personal Christian life. It helps us to rear our children well and gives us all the instruction we need for a successful prayer life. And most of all it teaches us how to protect ourselves from the enemy of our soul. Amen

# The Anointing Oil

*Then the Lord said to Moses, "Take the following fine spices: 500 shekels of liquid myrrh, half as much (that is, 250 shekels) of fragrant cinnamon, 250 shekels of fragrant calamus, 500 shekels of cassia – all according to the sanctuary shekel and a hin of olive oil. Make these into a sacred anointing oil, a fragrant blend, the work of a perfumer. It will be the sacred anointing oil* (Exodus 30:22-25).

The ingredients of the anointing oil found in Exodus show us some fascinating biblical types. God always has a reason for his instructions, and I have found it an absorbing task to search out possible reasons behind these ingredients he instructed the Israelites to use for the anointing oil. In the Old Testament this special mixture was used to anoint the High Priest and his sons, the altar, and those things that were to be set apart for use in the Tabernacle.

> Drops of Myrrh can be accelerated by wounding the tree with a knife.

The first ingredient is liquid Myrrh, obtained from the sap and resin of the Myrrh tree. Stones are placed under the tree and the resin falls naturally from the branches to harden on the stones beneath. The drops of Myrrh can be accelerated by wounding the tree by cutting the trunk and branches with a knife.

So, I understand that the wounding of the tree can indicate dramatically the suffering through which Christ was to pass during his trial and crucifixion.

The next, Cinnamon, comes from a tree that grows about thirty feet high and bears small white flowers on spreading branches. The oil is distilled from the bark after it has been softened by soaking in sea water. Today cinnamon is not liked as a scent, but the Hebrews thought it a glorious scent.

Cinnamon has recently been discovered as a healing agent and those with ailments are urged to use it extensively. So, here we can see the transcending healing power of God being included in the anointing oil.

There are two more ingredients, scent plants such as Sweet Cane and Cassia. Sweet Cane *(corus calamus)*, commonly known as sweet flag or calamus is a tall perennial wetland plant with scented leaves and more strongly scented rhizomes which have been used for medicine. Probably indigenous to India it is now found across Europe, in southern Russia, northern Asia Minor, southern Siberia, China, Indonesia, Japan, Burma, Sri Lanka, Australia, as well as southern Canada and Northern USA.

Cassia - The cinnamon cassia came over the Indian ocean to South Arabia, and so up by caravan to Palestine. (Ex 30:24; Ezekiel 27:19). There is some argument as to whether this cassia is the same as the cinnamon in Song of Solomon, and also in Revelation 18:13. The Cassia in Psalm 45:8 uses a different Hebrew word and is thought to be orrisroot. This produces a well-known scent used even today in the temples of India.

These two scents, so much loved by the Israelite people, are liberally sprinkled throughout the Song of Solomon, long considered to be a picture of the relationship between Christ and his church. The Psalms also speak of perfumes as being associated with Christ as the bridegroom of the Christian church (Psalm 45:8).

> It is possible to produce twenty gallons
> of oil from one olive tree.

The last ingredient is Olive oil. Olive trees are found all over Palestine. They grow well by the sea. Only one flower in every hundred produces fruit. So, there is an overflowing abundance of flowers but still plenty of fruit. It is possible to produce twenty gallons of oil from one olive tree.

When harvested the branches are shaken or beaten. The oil is full of goodness and healing. These facts speak to us once again of God's abundant supply of healing power (James 5:14).

One of the instructions for the consecration of the High Priest was to pour the anointing oil over his head. Psalm 133 mentions the anointing oil poured on Aaron's head.

*How good and pleasant it is when God's people live together in unity! It is like precious oil poured on the head, running down on the beard, running down on Aaron's beard, down on the collar of his robe. It is as if the dew of Hermon were falling on Mt Zion. For there the LORD bestows his blessing, even life forevermore.*

The anointing oil is also like the pure dew of heaven falling on Mount Hermon and running down the slopes, slowly gathering into streams of water. Which in turn become a mighty river of blessing and eternal life.

So, we can see the anointing oil points to Jesus, his sufferings for us, the sweetness of his presence and his purity. It is an oil that has healing properties. It is an oil that is given in abundance. We need to thank God for his great knowledge and foresight in choosing the ingredients of the anointing oil to point to the wonder and suffering of our Saviour, and our healing, abundance, protection and unity.

Earlier Moses had been instructed to anoint Aaron and his sons with the blood of the sacrifice on the tip of the right ear, on the right thumb and on the big toe of the right foot. This anointing pointed to protection from sin through things we hear, from sin through things we can touch, and from sin through wrong living. If we have accepted Jesus as our Saviour, the result is we are anointed to live right and to do good each day. This anointing is to keep us pure in our walk with God.

However, here Moses consecrates the priests with the anointing oil, setting them apart for the service of God.

*Anoint Aaron and his sons and consecrate them so they may serve me as priests. Say to the Israelites, "This is to be my sacred anointing oil for the generations to come. Do not pour it on anyone else's body and do not make any other oil using the same formula. It is sacred, and you are to consider it sacred. Whoever makes perfume like it and puts it on anyone other than a priest must be cut off from their people"* (Exodus 30:30-33).

Under the New Covenant we too are priests. We too are set apart, sanctified for service to God, as the apostle Peter makes clear.

*"But you are a chosen people, a royal priesthood, a holy nation, God's special possession, that you may declare the praises of him who called you out of darkness into his wonderful light"* (1 Peter 2:9).

**Heavenly Father**, thank you for this precious anointing oil and for the purpose it fulfills. Thank you for its teaching. You always have a purpose in every instruction you give, and this is no exception. May the symbolism here help us to understand the sufferings of Jesus and the way he brings healing and health and unity to the body of Christ as a whole. Help us to be careful to monitor what we hear, what we touch, and the places we go in our daily living. May we be willing to be set apart, anointed by you, for service in whatever area you choose. Amen

# The Second Coming

*Look, he is coming with the clouds, and every eye will see him, even those who pierced him, and all peoples on earth will mourn because of him. So shall it be. Amen* (Revelation 1:7).

Martin Luther had a remarkable view of the return of Christ. One that is sure to keep us expectant and ready for that day of the Lord:

"Live as if Christ died yesterday, rose this morning and is coming back tomorrow."

We live in exciting yet terrible times. For the first time in history circumstances are pointing to the possible end of the human race. Surely God will not allow man to go too far in his desire to interfere with the building blocks of life, with our very DNA? But it seems already scientists have started to manipulate the DNA of a nucleus in a Petrie dish. They may have a noble aim, to eradicate disease, but they are dealing with the fabric of life itself.

I remember when the first baby was formed in a Petrie dish and placed in a mother's womb. I remember wondering would this baby have a soul? A daughter was born, and she grew up as a perfectly normal girl which was a relief to me. Then a sheep was cloned and who knows what may be going on now, decades later, in scientific laboratories in countries like communist China.

Experiments are no doubt being conducted in secret by scientists who do not believe there is a god to whom they will eventually have to give account of their actions.

Personally, I believe that Jesus must come soon. There are definite signs of the end of this world system and the winding up of history.

First, the return of the Jews to their ancestral homeland. Israel is promised restoration in the last days.

*He will bring you to the land that belonged to your ancestors, and you will take possession of it. He will make you (the returned Israel of the last days) more prosperous and numerous than your ancestors* (Deuteronomy 30:5).

The formation of Israel in 1948 was this fulfillment of Isaiah's prophecy:

*Can a country be born in a day or a nation brought forth in a moment? Yet no sooner is Zion in labour than she gives birth to her children* (Isaiah 66:8).

Second, is the fact that in recent years many thousands of Jews have accepted Jesus Christ as their Messiah. In the book of Zechariah, we see a prophecy he wrote concerning this wonderful news.

*And I will pour out on the house of David and the inhabitants of Jerusalem a spirit of grace and supplication. They will look on me, the one they have pierced, and they will mourn for him as one mourns for an only child. And grieve bitterly for him as one who grieves for a firstborn son* (Zechariah 12:10).

Jewish people accepting Jesus as their Messiah is a sign the end is near, and today in Israel there are over 150 congregations of Jewish Christian believers. Also, many hundreds of thousands of Jews living throughout the world now claim Jesus as their Messiah.

We look forward to the day of the Lord when every eye will see Jesus coming in the clouds and the dead will rise up from their graves to meet the Lord in the air. Those who are still living on that day will join them, being changed in the twinkling of an eye. What a marvellous miracle that will be and what a glorious time of praise and worship will follow.

> *But your dead will live, LORD;*
> *their bodies will rise – let those*
> *who dwell in the dust wake up*
> *and shout for joy – your dew is*
> *like the dew of the morning; the*
> *earth will give birth to her dead*
> (Isaiah 26:19).

**Heavenly Father**, you are the only one who knows what the future holds. We must trust you for the future of our family and for the future of our nation and indeed for the future of the whole of this planet of ours. Thank you that you are the Almighty God and that you have everything under your control. Nothing can happen unless you allow it. This gives us contentment while we wait patiently for the future to be made plain to us. We live in exciting but perilous times waiting and trusting you to gain ultimate victory over all the powers of evil. Little by little we know your purposes will be worked out and Jesus will come as promised. May we be ready for that great day. Amen

# Chosen by God

*"An angel of the Lord appeared to them, and the glory of the Lord shone around them, and they were terrified. But the angel said. I bring you good news of great joy that will be for all people"* (Luke 2:9-10).

I asked myself the question. Why were the shepherds chosen by God to be the first to see the baby Jesus? My first thought was they were nearby, they were available, and they were awake! Then I thought how appropriate that shepherds were chosen to be the first to worship the King, because Jesus was to be the Lamb of God sent to die to take away the sins of the world.

Why were they chosen? They were shepherds, not considered clean enough to attend the temple services, but evidently God looked on their hearts and deemed them worthy to hear the wonderful news of the birth of the baby in Bethlehem.

Shepherds, as a group, were brave, they had to protect their flocks from predators. They had character and were caring and faithful. Shepherding was a great preparation to be a leader in Israel as we can see from the lives of Moses and David

The shepherds were blessed because they believed the proclamation of the angelic host and they acted accordingly. They ran to see the baby, born and laid in a manger as the angels had told them and they worshiped him, their Saviour and Messiah.

Then the shepherds *"returned, glorifying and praising God for all the things they had heard and seen which were just as they had been told"*.

Why were they chosen by God? According to William Barclay, these shepherds cared for the flocks belonging to the priests. The lambs they cared for were to be sacrificed on the temple mount. William Barclay says,

> "The shepherds were despised by the orthodox good people of the day. Shepherds were quite unable to keep the details of the ceremonial law; they could not observe all the meticulous hand washings and rules and regulations. Their flocks made far too many constant demands on them; and so, the orthodox looked down on them as very common people. It was to these simple men of the fields that God's message first came...

> "It is most likely that these shepherds were in charge of the flocks from which the temple offerings were chosen. It is a lovely thought that the shepherds who looked after the temple lambs were the first to see the Lamb of God."

Bethlehem was only six miles from the temple in Jerusalem and the priests needed many lambs for sacrifices. On most days a male lamb without blemish was sacrificed every morning and another every evening but on special days there were far more sacrifices offered. God knew the hearts of these special shepherds and he allowed them to be the first to see Mary's babe, born to be our Saviour.

**Heavenly Father,** thank you for the shepherds who heard your message so long ago and for their willingness to obey the angels. Even though they were outwardly imperfect, yet you could see their hearts were brave and true. In the same way, we know that you don't look on our outward appearance, but you look on our heart to see if we are loving you and following you sincerely. May we always obey your voice when you reveal it to us through your Word or through the still small voice of the Holy Spirit. And may we, like the shepherds, be willing to testify to the great things you have done. Amen

# Changing the Culture

Jesus gave his disciples this charge: *"God authorised me to commission you: Go out and train everyone you meet, far and near, in this way of life, marking them by baptism in the three-fold name Father, Son and Holy Spirit. Then instruct them in the practice of all I have commanded you. I'll be with you as you do this, day after day after day, right up to the end of the age"* (Matthew 28:18-20 The Message Bible).

Luke's gospel was written to the Greeks who had a similar culture to the one we have today. Humanism has degraded our culture by abandoning the Judeo/Christian foundation that I remember from my teenage years in the 1940's. Now we have a lust driven society, with violence against women increasing and honour and truth being laid aside. Many in spheres of influence, such as judges, lawyers, teachers, members of parliament, and journalists have been educated by humanist teachers who have infiltrated the universities.

Humanists teach that everyone can decide what is right for themselves and can do whatever feels good to them, so long as they do not hurt anyone else. In fact, we are back to the time of the Old Testament book of Judges, 21:25, *"In those days Israel had no king; everyone did as they saw fit."*

Decisions have been made and laws have been passed which go a long way toward destroying our culture, our society, our families and therefore our nation.

One way to change a culture is to change the meaning of words. So, now we have "wicked" meaning "good" and vice versa, along with the era of the anti-hero where the evil man is the hero of the story. The prophet Isaiah foresaw this era, *"Woe to those who call evil good, and good evil, who put darkness for light and light for darkness, who put bitter for sweet and sweet for bitter* (Isaiah 5:20).

The ordinary man and woman feels helpless to change any of this deterioration of our culture. But, as Edmund Burke said, "All it takes for evil to succeed is for good men to do nothing," so we need to do something if we can. [20]

The way ordinary people can effect change is by courageously speaking to our members of parliament, our local councils, and our Parents and Friends Associations. Those who are talented speakers should try for office in organisations such as Rotary which seeks to accomplish good in the world.

If we do nothing, then nothing will change. Prayer will help and God can turn things around, but only if we are willing to leave our church ghetto (safe place) and get out into the real world where we can effect change. Revival would be a help, but it is not enough to change individuals we need reformation of the government, the judicial system, the universities, the schools, the news services, and indeed all aspects of the nation.

Because of the gradual weakening of the Christian church in Australia many people are untaught in the Word of God. This lack of scripture knowledge results in the bullying and nastiness of many school children, showing a sad lack of character. Character traits preferred include such things as honesty, kindness, courage and self-control.

---

[20] Edmund Burke 1729-1797 British statesman and political thinker.

Luke's gospel is a good tool to reach the ordinary men and women who have not heard the story of Jesus and the salvation he offers. The government allows Scripture classes in secular schools, so parents have the choice of sending their children into Scripture classes or Ethics classes. But those who attend Ethics classes don't have the chance to hear the Bible stories or the truth of the Good News of the gospel which could lead to the development of Christian virtues.

Up until the 1950's we had a society where children were taught the Ten Commandments and authority figures were respected and admired. Children were taught to honour their parents and were mostly obedient to them and to their teachers.

In 2021 we have a society where many individuals are doing what seems right to them and teaching their children without a Judeo/Christian foundation. But children who are not taught the Ten Commandments will be stealing and lying by the time they are ten years of age, with no understanding that this is wrong![21]

Think of the savings that would occur in a society in which everyone was completely honest! Shop keepers could reduce their prices as there would be no shop lifting. There would be less need for police and less gaols, thus saving government money for more necessary things such as hospitals, schools, roads and bridges.

---

[21] Unfortunately, I have lost the source of this quote.

What a utopia we would have if everyone lived by the Word of God in obedience to him. As Christians we should be thinking of what we can do to influence our culture and to reach out into the community. With God's help we must learn how to make a difference to our neighbours and to our schools and our local councils. We cannot stay safely in our Christian ghetto (our church) and pray for people to come to us we must reach out and prove that we have the answers to the distress we see around us.

**Heavenly Father** help us and direct us in ways we can be useful in turning our culture back to the Judeo/Christian foundations. Give us strong, honest politicians who will pass laws for the good of all Australians. Give us strong pastors who will courageously stand for Christian virtues and teach their congregations to make a difference in the culture. Give us a new generation of Elijah's who will turn the children back to their fathers and so make way for a wonderful revival and reformation of our nation. Amen.

# The Golden Rule

Jesus said, *"Do unto others as you would have them do unto you."*

Jesus made this rule because he wants each of us to have a happy life, a good family life and many friends.

The Golden Rule means many things, some of them are:

- ⚕ If you want others to love you then you must be loving toward them.
- ⚕ If you want others to be kind to you then you must be kind to them.
- ⚕ If you want others to be patient with you then you must be patient with them.
- ⚕ If you want others to use good manners toward you then you must use good manners toward them.
- ⚕ If you want others to forgive you when you hurt them, then you must forgive them when they hurt you.
- ⚕ If you want others to keep control of their emotions, then you must try hard to keep control of your emotions as well.

*"Don't think that friendship authorizes you to say disagreeable things to your intimate friends. The nearer you come into relationship with a person the more necessary tact and courtesy become."*
(Oliver Wendell Holmes)

If, instead of being loving and kind, you are unloving, unkind, impatient, bad-mannered, unforgiving and un-controlled then not many will like you and you won't have many friends.

If you find it hard to be loving, kind, patient, good-mannered, forgiving and self-controlled in your emotions then ask God to help you.

He will help you if you ask him sincerely with all your heart.

**Heavenly Father**, please help us to be loving, kind and patient within the family circle. Help us to remember that it is more important to have good manners within the family than with our friends or with strangers. Help us to forgive when other people hurt our feelings even as you forgive us for the many times we sin and fall short of the mark. Most of all help us to have good self-control in our life, especially in the way we deal with other people. Show us how to do something toward changing our culture Even if we can only influence a few people the ideas we share could spread and grow. Amen.

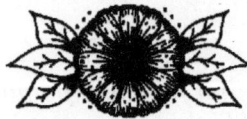

# The Courage of Jesus

*Who is this coming from Edom, from Bozrah, with his garments stained crimson? Who is this robed in splendour, striding forward in the greatness of his strength? "It is I, proclaiming victory, mighty to save" (Isaiah 63:1.)*

There are several verses in Isaiah that prophesy about the courage and strength of Jesus our Saviour. Here we read of his triumph over Satan and the redemption he wrought for us all.

I have always been overawed at the courage of Jesus, knowing that he must have seen many crucifixions in his time while being aware that one day he would have to face the same fate. Until recently I did not realise just how many of these crucifixions he would have seen and heard. William Baxter states in his commentary on Luke's Gospel: -

> "When Jesus was around eleven years of age a man known as Judas the Galilean led a rebellion against Rome. He attacked the royal armoury in Sepphoris which was only 4 miles from Nazareth. The Roman vengeance was swift and sudden. Sepphoris was burned to the ground and the inhabitants were sold as slaves. Then 2,000 of the rebels were crucified on crosses which were set up along the roadside as a warning to others."

So, Jesus saw all the agonies of crucifixion and yet bravely went ahead with his ministry, knowing that he too would have to suffer this terrible death.

He did it to accomplish our salvation and how grateful we are for his courage and sacrifice for us.

**Heavenly Father**, how grateful we are that Jesus was willing to endure the cross for us. We are overwhelmed by the wonder of the victory won through his suffering. Thank you for the grace and mercy freely given to everyone who accepts the sacrifice made by Jesus for their sins to be forgiven. Help us to be always aware of what Jesus did for us and to be grateful to him. Amen

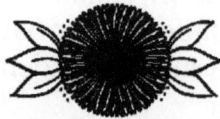

# A Servant Attitude

*Then an angel of the Lord appeared to him standing at the right side of the altar of incense. When Zechariah saw him, he was startled and was gripped with fear. But the angel said to him: Do not be afraid, Zechariah; your prayer has been heard. Your wife Elizabeth will bear you a son, and you are to call him John. He will be a joy and delight to you, and many will rejoice because of his birth, for he will be great in the sight of the Lord* (Luke 1:11-15).

Zechariah's wife Elizabeth must have suffered during the years she was barren. At first her women friends would have taunted her, asking when she intended to start having a family. Slowly over the years the hurtful comments would have changed to pitying glances as she remained barren. The years passed slowly. Married at around fifteen or sixteen years of age, as was the custom, Elizabeth would have suffered disappointment after disappointment. Finally, after a lifetime of hoping she knew that her time for childbearing was almost gone, but she and Zechariah kept on praying for a child.

Her husband Zechariah, who belonged to the priestly division of Abijah, loved his wife dearly and would not listen to reproaches of Elizabeth from his relatives. Even though it was extremely important for Jewish men to have a son to carry on the family name he did not show his wife any less devotion but proved himself a loving and caring husband.

These two people observed all the Lord's commands and decrees blamelessly. They were both righteous in God's eyes. Elizabeth would have busied herself with acts of charity among the widows and orphans of the village, but she would have had time for meditation on the scrolls her husband Zechariah made available to her. Because of this she was aware that the time was approaching for the Messiah of Israel to be born into the world.

It is with this background that Zechariah went up to Jerusalem to fulfil his obligation to serve in the temple. On the day he was chosen by lot to go into the temple to burn incense all the assembled worshipers were praying in the outer court. Zechariah's vision and the instructions he was given caused great excitement in his heart. In great trepidation he travelled home to share with Elizabeth what had happened. He could not speak so had to write her notes about his experience.

She was overjoyed and embraced the message of the angel through her husband. In due course the words the angel had spoken came true. Elizabeth became pregnant and, not wanting to become a figure of fun to her contemporaries she hid herself until her time should come.

When she was about six months pregnant Mary, one of her relatives from Nazareth, came to visit. As soon as Elisabeth saw Mary her babe jumped for joy in her womb, and she knew that Mary was the one chosen to bear the Messiah of Israel.

What a time of rejoicing and enjoying sweet fellowship they must have had together. Mary drew strength from Elizabeth. It was wonderful to her that she had been told by the angel Gabriel that Elizabeth was pregnant. This strengthened her faith, that the Lord was indeed with her also and that, although still a virgin, she was bearing a babe who would be called the Son of God.

The time came for Elizabeth to bear her son and her relatives gathered around to suggest names, but Zechariah agreed with his wife that the babe's name would be John. Immediately his tongue was loosed, and he began to praise God.

**Heavenly Father,** thank you for Zachariah and Elizabeth, this faithful couple who persevered in prayer until you granted their request. What a wonderful task you gave them to bring into the world the babe who was to become John the Baptist, the herald of our Saviour, Jesus the Messiah, who came into this world to make sacrifice for our sins. Help us too, to persevere in our prayers until we receive an answer from you. We know that sometimes the answer will be, "Yes", your prayer is granted" but at other times, "No" or perhaps, "Wait a while." We pray you will always help us to persevere faithfully in our prayers until we receive an answer from you. Amen

# The Kingdom of God

*In the time of those kings, the God of heaven will set up a kingdom that will never be destroyed, nor will it be left to another people. It will crush all those kingdoms and bring them to an end, but it will itself endure forever* (Daniel 2:44).

In Daniel we read of the rock, cut out, but not by human hands, that destroys Nebuchadnezzar's image which represents the nations of the world

When Jesus came, he preached a different kind of Kingdom. This was to be a kingdom of love, living in the hearts of those who accepted him and lived in obedience to him as the Son of God, their Saviour.

Why are none of our modern nations mentioned in Daniel's figure?

Because the modern nations that we know all came into being after the Kingdom of God began. As we are told in Da 2:35b *"the rock that struck the statue became a huge mountain and filled the whole earth."*

We are still waiting for God to fulfil this prophecy, to fill the whole earth with his Kingdom. But there is a task for us to complete first. We are still a long way from completing the commission Jesus gave us to go into the world and make disciples. This is our task, but we are still a long way from fulfilling it.

Part of the reason is the present state of the church. Here is a quote from the book *The Kingdom of God* written sometime after the Second World War which still speaks with clarity to us today.

"The church lives in tension between the victory won in Christ and a victory anything but won, between a kingdom which is present and which we may enter and a kingdom we can neither be, nor create.

"We must live as though Christ will come today! This gives us a sense of urgency which springs from a sense of impending judgment.

"For we know, if we are not blind, that a society that has flouted the law of God and placed gain above rectitude, that has worshipped a sorry procession of false gods dressed up in jack boots, that has defaced and violated the creature made in the divine image, that has been vaguely religious in a sentimental sort of way yet has cared for nothing so much as its material comfort, is under indictment.

"That society must now stand in history and show cause why it should continue to exist! This judgment hangs over us; we do not know how to save ourselves from it, frantically though we try. And it is in this context of desperation that the church today speaks – the gospel of end time urgency." [22]

---

[22] Quote from *The Kingdom of God* by John Bright, Pg. 247-248

**Heavenly Father**, we pray that more and more Christians will be moved to help fulfill the Great Commission so that the Kingdom of God will indeed fill the whole earth. We pray for a revival of a fear and respect for God which seems to be sadly lacking today. Thank you for the beginnings of such a revival and pray that it will be increased throughout the earth. Amen

# Thoughts on The Passover

*When you enter the land that the LORD will give you as he promised, observe this ceremony. And when your children ask you, "What does this ceremony mean to you." Then tell them, "It is the Passover sacrifice to the LORD who passed over the houses of the Israelites in Egypt and spared our homes when he struck down the Egyptians"* (Exodus 12:25-26).

In the celebration of the Passover there were some very interesting types present in the feast.

A bowl of salt water represented the tears that were shed by the Israelites, and bitter herbs represented the slavery they endured. A paste they called "charoseth" consisting of apples, dates, pomegranates and nuts indicated the bricks made in Egypt, and sticks of cinnamon indicated the straw.

The four cups of wine stood for the four promises of Exodus 6:6-7.

- ✿ "I will bring you out from under the burdens of the Egyptians."
- ✿ "I will rid you of their bondage."
- ✿ "I will redeem you with an outstretched arm."
- ✿ "I will take you as my own people, and I will be your God."

The Israelites then sang the "Hallel" (Praise God), Psalms 113-118, as these were an essential part of the Passover Feast.

The Great Hallel that was sung at the conclusion of the Passover is Psalm 136. This was the Psalm sung by Jesus and the disciples on their way to the garden of Gethsemane. The message of this Psalm, *"His love endures forever,"* is sung over and over again.

There in the Garden long ago, Jesus wrestled in prayer, and the journey to our salvation began in earnest.

**Heavenly Father,** how wonderful that Jesus was determined to follow your will and was willing to proceed to the cross for our salvation even though he knew that decision was to bring great agony and suffering. Thank you too, for this memorial of the Passover, reminding us of the way you protected your people and delivered them from Egypt. Thank you that you are still protecting your people and delivering them when they look to you in faith. Help us to always believe in your great love and compassion toward us, your children. Amen

www.ingramcontent.com/pod-product-compliance
Lightning Source LLC
Chambersburg PA
CBHW022010090426
42741CB00007B/974